GOD IS CLOSER THAN YOU THINK

God Is Closer
than You Think

Juan Carlos Ortiz

Servant Publications
Ann Arbor, Michigan

Unless otherwise noted, Scripture quotations are taken from the New
American Standard Bible © THE LOCKMAN FOUNDATION 1960,
1962, 1963, 1968, 1971, 1972, 1973, 1975, 1977. All rights reserved.

Vine Books is an imprint of Servant Publications especially designed
to serve Evangelical Christians.

Published by Servant Publications
P.O. Box 8617
Ann Arbor, Michigan 48107

Cover design by Gerald L. Gawronski / The Look

92 93 94 95 96 97 98   10 9 8 7 6 5 4 3 2 1

Printed in the United States of America
ISBN 0-89283-799-3

Library of Congress Cataloging-in-Publication Data

Ortiz, Juan Carlos, 1934–
    God is closer than you think / Juan Carlos Ortiz.
        p. cm.
    ISBN 0-89283-799-3
    1. Spiritual life. 2. Prayer. I. Title.
    BV4501.2.O7246 1992
    248.4—dc20   92-24869

Contents

Foreword

Many of us have questions regarding prayer that we hesitate to ask: How many times must I repeat the same prayer? Will God really give me everything I ask for? If I pray for the salvation of others, will God make it impossible for them to resist? Is prayer like money with which to buy blessings from God? Would a half hour of prayer grant me more blessings than fifteen minutes? Why do I ask and ask and still not receive? What does it mean to pray without ceasing? How can I receive an answer to more of my prayers? What can I do to make my prayer life a pleasurable experience? Why is it that sometimes the only answer to my prayers is silence?

Dr. Ortiz treats these questions with extraordinary audacity. His childhood home was a house of prayer. His mother and his four brothers and sisters are all preachers. During his boyhood, adolescence, and youth, there were prayer vigils in his home from Friday evening until dawn on Saturday.

Juan Carlos Ortiz is an authority on prayer. He has engaged in fasting, spiritual warfare, contemplation, and meditation. He has prayed in silence, aloud, alone on a mountaintop, in prayer chains, with charismatic groups, in monasteries, and with the sick. In this book he shares many of his experiences, both positive and negative, offering fresh insight into a life of intimacy with God.

He is also a pastor and counselor. He has shared with those who suffer and those who seek God for solutions to their problems and difficulties. In this book, he confronts the challenge of prayer in a practical and honest way, responding to the doubts and obstacles of all sincere believers.

As you open these pages, you will find that Juan Carlos Ortiz challenges some of your traditional beliefs. On other pages, he will make you laugh at yourself. But more than anything, you will learn how to make prayer the most desired and pleasant experience of your life! *God Is Closer than You Think* will clear your mind regarding prayer. It will take away any guilt regarding not "praying enough," and it will enable you to grow strong in your relationship with God.

—Dr. Robert H. Schuller
Founding Pastor,
The Crystal Cathedral

1 || *God Is on the Inside*

"**A**TTENTION!" cried the wild-eyed man in the Judean wilderness. "The kingdom of heaven is close at hand. You had better repent if you know what's good for you."

John the Baptist was not like every other Jew. Dressed in camel's hair, living off the desert land, he still managed to draw ordinary, respectable people from Jerusalem, and from even farther afield. Some confessed their sins and were baptized. They were the lucky ones—they believed that John was right about the kingdom of heaven.

John's vindication came when the Messiah arrived, seeking baptism. Heaven was opened and the Holy Spirit came down like a dove, settling on the Nazarene carpenter. Then a voice from above said: "This is My beloved Son, in whom I am well-pleased" (Matthew 3:17).

From then on, the kingdom grew. There were no

boundary lines, no citizenship papers, no city ramparts being raised. But if you could have taken a census of the spirit, you would have discovered a strange thing, more bizarre than any science fiction story: this uncrowned king was leaving pieces of himself, spiritual seeds, in each one of his followers. The seeds were growing. In fact, they could not die as long as their hosts nurtured them.

Jesus the man died. He rose and appeared to many, and soon made a physical exit. His kingdom remained. Not in buildings, not in military might, not in a civil government, but in the same place it had begun—in the hearts of men and women.

This would have been an unfathomable mystery, but God decided to let his people in on the secret. Paul explained to the Colossians that God commissioned him to "fully carry out the preaching of the word of God, that is, the mystery which has been hidden from the past ages and generations; but has not been manifested to His saints, to whom God willed to make known what is the riches of the glory of this mystery among the Gentiles, which is Christ in you, the hope of glory" (Colossians 1:25-27).

Christ in you, the hope of glory. The hope of the Father, the hope of the angels, the hope of the prophets, the hope of the kingdom of God is Christ *in us.* The ages and the generations before Jesus all pointed to that day when God would stake his claim not in piles of rocks, or in a cloud-covered mountain, or in a lavish temple, but in the hearts of his people. Now he's done that. Christ is not borrowing our hearts for a few months, or once a week. He has transformed us into owner-occupied dwellings.

And that's all this book is about—*Christ living in us,*

Christ speaking with us, Christ at work in us. Nothing scary, nothing unattainable, nothing somber. Quite the opposite. We will explore the living engine God has set up inside flesh and bone, expanding the kingdom already at hand. Paul said "it is God who is at work in you, both to will and to work for His good pleasure" (Philippians 2:13). Do you want God's good purposes to rise to the surface in your life? Then acknowledge that he's there to begin with.

HIDE AND SEEK

In the Old Testament, God was elsewhere. I'm not sure anybody knew exactly where he was, but they knew he wasn't walking around Judea and Samaria. "I will lift *up* my eyes to the mountains," it was said. "Lift *up* your hands to the sanctuary." The earth was the footstool for his feet, but where exactly was his chair? Of course, God was in heaven, but where was heaven besides up?

Since God was distant, if you wanted him, you had to look hard to find him. To make matters worse, you never knew if he would answer your call. "Seek the Lord while He may be found" (Isaiah 55:6).

But when you found him—or, when he found you—you had better be sure your face was clean and your tithes paid. He would visit in the form of wind, fire, lightning. He didn't shirk at getting attention with a big booming noise or voice. His people were content to be insulated from this deity: "Talk to Moses first, yes, then he can tell us what you said." When God thundered, no one needed persuading to stay off the foot of the holy mountain. God was a mystery, a distant mystery.

Jesus' coming changed all that. It didn't change the Father, who contains at once mercy and judgment, loving kindness and awesome power. But Jesus introduced a new dimension to the relationship between the Father and his people. Before, people were always *seeking* God; now it became a matter of *having* God's presence. God visited with a whirlwind in the Old Testament, but in Jesus he came quietly to sit down beside us.

Awareness of this difference consumed the author of Hebrews:

> For if that first covenant had been faultless, there would have been no occasion sought for a second. For finding fault with them, He says, "Behold, days are coming, says the Lord, when I will effect a new cove-nant with the house of Israel and with the house of Judah; not like the covenant which I made with their fathers on the day when I took them by the hand to lead them out of the land of Egypt; for they did not continue in My covenant, and I did not care for them, says the Lord. For this is the covenant that I will make with the house of Israel after those days, says the Lord: I will put My laws into their minds, and I will write them upon their hearts. **Hebrews 8:7-10**

The laws were no longer to be love letters from a God in another universe, chiseled into a rock or scrawled on a scroll. Instead, God's heart and his will for his people would be put right inside them. The laws would not sim-ply be passed through one ear into the memory, where they could easily slip out the other ear. They would be written onto the hearts of men and women. And from those transformed hearts, from within, God would reveal himself. The author of Hebrews continued:

> And I will be their God, and they shall be My people. And they shall not teach everyone His fellow-citizen, and everyone his brother, saying, "Know the Lord," for all shall know Me, from the least to the greatest of them. For I will be merciful to their iniquities, and I will remember their sins no more." When He said, "A new covenant," He has made the first obsolete. But whatever is becoming obsolete and growing old is ready to disappear. **Hebrews 8:10-13**

The Law of Moses was good—good for that time. It was a shadow cast by God's pure light of eternity falling across something not fully seen or understood, something in the future spoken of by the prophets. We know now that that something was the New Covenant. Once Jesus established it, the old one became obsolete. It didn't break, or even become outdated. It was a wonderful covenant, authored by God, that passed from the present into history when a superior agreement took effect.

The main difference was that God no longer dwelt in the shadows. He was distant before, but now, as children of light, we find that he has taken up residence not just in our midst, but inside our hearts.

LIVING STONES

The old tabernacle and the old temple of Solomon were strictly for God, not his people. The tabernacle was only seventy-five feet by 150 feet; the people numbered in the millions. Not exactly room enough to pack people in for a nice Sabbath ceremony, even if you scheduled an early and late service. There were no benches, no pews. No, the emphasis was on the altar, on the sacrifices, and on the Holy of Holies. The sacrifices ushered in God, who showed up with fire to reveal his presence with his people.

Those buildings symbolized the true building that Jesus would build. When Jesus spoke with the Samaritan woman at the well, she engaged him in a debate about whether true worship should take place at Mount Gerizim or in Jerusalem. He had a surprise answer: neither one. "But an hour is coming, and now is, when the true worshipers shall worship the Father in spirit and truth; for such people the Father seeks to be His worshipers" (John 4:23).

I can envision Jesus in Jerusalem, rubbing his hands across those massive stones of the temple, fully aware that it embodied one of history's greatest turning points. "Dear temple, until now you have been a symbol of the temple I am going to build. Now that time is at hand. Thank you for your ministry, for foreshadowing the great work the Father has planned. And goodbye."

After running the riffraff out of the temple, Jesus had a little fun confounding the Jews who were demanding a miracle to prove his authority. "Destroy this temple, and I will raise it again in three days," he said (John 2:19).

His enemies didn't understand this. I'm not sure many of us fully comprehend, either. Jesus was not simply spinning riddles about his death and his resurrection on the third day. He was talking about a building without bricks, a structure without stones, a building adhesive stronger than mortar. Jesus spoke of his body, which is you and me. It's a building made of living stones.

On Pentecost, he inaugurated that new building. As in the Old Testament inaugurations, there was fire from heaven. This time it came not on the roof of the building, but on the "roof" of the people, tongues of fire over their heads. God was saying, "From now on, I will dwell here, among people." That's why the primitive church didn't bother with church buildings. They understood the transition from the old system to the new. They didn't want to turn back the clock. They took the presence of God with them wherever they went.

STILL AT HAND

What about us—are we taking God with us wherever we go? Or have our church buildings, so big and beautiful, so full of teaching and warm worship, deceived us into thinking God checked out of our little bodies for a long stay at the big cathedral?

Perhaps we need to reflect on the message brought by John the Baptist. We must understand that he was no carnival huckster offering a temporary bargain: "Step right up! The kingdom of heaven is at hand. Hurry, sign up for your memberships while they last! You won't find this deal offered in Bethany or Bethsaida. No, sir, the kingdom of heaven—for a limited time only, here at the Jordan River."

I suspect that all Christians believe, or would say they believe, that Christ dwells in us, that the kingdom of heaven extends into our regenerated spirits. Yet we don't all act like it. We treat God as if he's far away—sleeping peacefully in heaven, or on vacation until his next guest appearance at church on Sunday. Jesus may have finished his appointed time on earth, but the at-hand kingdom did not dissolve after Easter or Pentecost. The same one who proclaimed that the kingdom was at hand also prophesied the coming of the Holy Spirit: "He who is coming after me is mightier than I, and I am not even fit to remove His sandals; He Himself will baptize you with the Holy Spirit and fire" (Matthew 3:11). When Jesus came, he elaborated: "I will ask the Father and He will give you another Helper, that He may be with you forever; that is the Spirit of truth, whom the world cannot receive, because it does not behold Him or know Him, but you know Him because He abides with you, and will be in you" (John 14:16-17). The kingdom was at hand. It still is. Jesus promised that when the Spirit comes, "He will guide you into all the truth; for He will not speak on His own initiative, but whatever He hears, He will speak; and He will disclose to you what is to come" (John 16:13).

So this is what Jesus has bequeathed to his followers: a guiding, speaking, disclosing, resident Counselor. Let's see what it means to turn him loose.

2 | *Permanent Power*

THE SAMARITAN WOMAN at the well was puzzled. Jews did not associate with Samaritans, yet here was this Jewish man asking her for a drink. Then the conversation began to get even stranger.

"If you knew the gift of God, and who it is who says to you, 'Give Me a drink,' you would have asked Him, and He would have given you living water," Jesus said.

"Living water" did not quite make sense to her, so she pointed out that Jesus had nothing to draw water with. But she was intrigued enough to ask, "Where can you get this living water?"

"Everyone who drinks of this water shall thirst again; but whoever drinks of the water that I shall give him shall never thirst; but the water that I shall give him shall become in him a well of water springing up to eternal life" (John 4:9-13).

A spring of eternal life! What a wonderful image of the new life bubbling inside of us! Not a stale, stagnant, dark well, requiring sweat and effort to get just a bucketful. But a spring of fresh water—gurgling up, flowing, running, cool and refreshing, as close as you want it, satisfying forever.

You don't have to own a special piece of real estate to have this lovely spring. If you've accepted Christ, you've automatically got it. Because that spiritual spring is in you, there is unlimited potential for what God can accomplish through you. He simply wants you to release the flow.

LETTING THE HELPER HELP

Let's continue to look at some differences between the Old and New Testament. The visitation of God in the Old Testament was often called "anointing." Priests had to be anointed. So did things. It was a temporary, performance-oriented situation, like a model putting on makeup. Anointing gives the impression of pouring oil, of empowering from *outside* over the head.

"Anoint" is not used much in Scripture after the resurrection. The comparable New Testament word is "filled." God's presence is no longer an off-and-on thing, but he comes to dwell continually. He does not come externally, but remains internally. He abides in us.

Now what exactly are we filled with? As we read in the last chapter, Jesus promised he would give us a helper when he left the earth. He did: the Holy Spirit. And he said the Spirit "will teach you all things."

All things? A tall order, but yes. We can better understand the potential of this by looking at Ezekiel 36:26-27. This was the Father's promise that was fulfilled at Pentecost, when the first New Testament outpouring of the Spirit occurred. "I will give you a new heart and put a new spirit within you; and I will remove the heart of stone from your flesh and give you a heart of flesh. And I will put My Spirit within you and cause you to walk in My statutes, and you will be careful to observe My ordinances."

The greatest problem of humankind, including the Israelites, had always been the inability to do God's will. Now here was a major change—something would cause the rebellious sons and daughters of Adam to follow God's laws. Who would initiate this strange occurrence? God, himself, through his indwelling Spirit.

Many Christians, though, expect something less when it comes to their potential for doing God's will. They are too quick to run up the white flag before the battle has begun. "We're all sinners," they say. "We may be spiritual, but we still carry around the flesh. I'm not perfect, just saved." There is some truth in all that. But you have to wonder, why did God give us his Spirit? Is it just so we can say, "I've got the Spirit"?

No. There are some very practical reasons. One is that *the Spirit will help us please God if we will trust him.* "And I will put My Spirit within you and cause you to walk in My statutes, and you will be careful to observe My ordinances." God promises me that I will be able to live the life that he wants me to live. Victorious living is possible after all.

In other words, we can be holy. This holiness is not a

matter of effort, but of grace. There's someone in us that moves us toward obedience to righteousness.

GRADUATING TO PROMISES

One reason we have this capacity to walk in righteousness lies in another change from Old Covenant to New Covenant—from commandments to promises. What were once laws handed down from on high, God promised to write in our hearts. He promised to place his Spirit inside us. With that Helper, he promised we would be careful to observe his ordinances.

This is how Peter described it:

His divine power has granted to us everything pertaining to life and godliness, through the true knowledge of Him who called us by His own glory and excellence. For by these He has granted to us His precious and magnificent promises, in order that by them you might become partakers of the divine nature, having escaped the corruption that is in the world by lust. 2 Peter 1:3-4

So now when I read, "Thou shalt not commit adultery," I read something like this: "God promises that I shall not commit adultery. God promises that my mind is redeemed and that when I see a beautiful woman, I can turn away or resist thoughts of the flesh." I am not saying a Spirit-filled Christian is immune to adultery, lust or any other temptation. But God has made a way out for us. One of his great promises, according to Peter, is that we can participate in God's own nature, which is divine, not fleshly. By doing that, we can escape the corruption that fills the world. Now some people don't want to escape. The lifeboat is right in front of them, but they choose to linger. They should not be surprised when they go down with the ship.

Some people get discouraged by the many commandments spread around the New Testament. "There's commandments here, commandments there. I thought we were under grace, not under the law." Well, we are under grace. Those commandments represent promises backed up by grace. The odds were stacked against anyone's complete obedience to the Law in the Old Testament. No more. The odds are in our favor because of him who lives in us, the one who makes obedience a natural thing. God wants our lives remolded in his image.

This grace, of course, does not give us permission to sin, even though we have the assurance of God's forgiveness if we confess. As Paul said, "Are we to continue in sin that grace might increase? May it never be! How shall we who died to sin still live in it?" (Romans 6:1-2). Rather, *grace is the ability that God gives us not to sin*. The focus is not on your effort to be a nice person. You cannot boast of your holiness because it is Christ at work through you.

POWER DRIVEN

When I was a teenager in Argentina, our old car had no power steering and no power brakes. We were just glad that it had an engine with power.

Once an American missionary was with me as I tried to squeeze into a downtown parking slot. I was grunting and sweating as I wrestled that steering wheel back and forth, trying to maneuver that big machine into a little space.

The missionary said, "Brother Ortiz, did you know that in America we have cars with power steering and power brakes?"

"Power steering?" I asked. "What is that?"

"You don't have to make any effort to turn the wheel," he said.

"No!" I said.

"The brakes, too," he said. "No effort to stop the car, either."

"How can this be?"

"Well, the engine makes the effort for you."

I still didn't believe him. But I thought, this man's a missionary—surely he's not lying. I didn't want to sound more ignorant than I already was, so I said nothing.

Still, I kept thinking. How does the engine know when I want to turn? Are Americans so technologically advanced that they have some remote sensor that enables the engine to know what you're thinking? But then what would happen if your attention drifts? The engine gets mixed signals; the car crashes. So much for fancy cars!

When I came to America a few years later, I drove a newer car. The first time I hit the brakes, my head hit the windshield. Then I understood that the missionary was right, only he had not explained it fully to me. I still had to make the decision to brake or to turn the wheel. The engine does the rest.

This is power. And this is how God's power works. We make a decision, we take a step, and God is faithful to kick in with us. When I say grace is the ability God gives us not to sin, I am talking about power. If we *choose* the godly path, he is there with power to help us walk it.

The element of choice, or free will, is important. God could have made us robots, programmed to obey and worship him. But this wouldn't have made much sense. It would be like you hearing a tape you recorded that says, "I love you. I love you. I love you" over and over again. Not much satisfaction there.

PERMANENT POWER

So I discovered power steering and power brakes. I also discovered that the automobile company did not put a switch on the dashboard enabling drivers to turn their power steering off and on. You can't find a button to turn the brakes from regular to power brakes. The auto makers knew that would be silly and more expensive, a big waste of design. The power is just there, waiting to be used.

Most Christians will tell you they have the power of God, but then they'll do something that betrays themselves.

Can you imagine praying like this: "Lord, enable me to love that no-good, cheating person. I can't do it on my own. Help me to love him." Then, to yourself, "Well, he hasn't given me any love yet. I feel the same way toward him as I did before praying."

So you try some more: "Oh, Lord, I need your love for this person." But your love account still feels empty. So you fail to love the one who offends you, and you imply that God is the guilty one because you prayed for love and he didn't give it to you.

Are you complete in Christ or not? You are looking for

something you already have. "The love of God has been poured out within our hearts through the Holy Spirit who was given to us" (Romans 5:5). Believe that when God requires something from you, you are able to do it!

It is a matter of using a little bit of will power to start. It is a matter of loving God so much that we want him to use us to further his kingdom, thereby creating the opportunity for God to accomplish things in us and through us. The process involves moving more and more in victory, not retreating, not doing only what it takes to barely escape the snatches of the evil one.

A 17-year-old boy in California asked me for prayer. I asked him why.

"I am ashamed to ask, but I will tell you anyway. You are a man, too," he said. "I want you to pray that the Lord takes away all my sexual desires."

"Why would you want that?" I asked.

"I want to live in holiness," he said. "Every time I see a nice girl, all these dirty things come to mind. I don't know what to do. So I want the Lord to deliver me from that desire."

"Listen, if I would pray that, and if God would answer the request, you would be abnormal," I replied. "When you see a pretty girl and all these thoughts come to you, just say, 'In the name of Jesus, no. God help me.' Just willingly touch the brake pedal in your thought machine, and God will push it till it stops."

Remember, God put a new heart in you. He deposited his Spirit, who will move you toward his will. God is waiting for you to tap that power brake, to flick your wrist and turn the power steering. You can opt for power or you can opt for weakness.

You can sing the hymn, "I am weak, Savior, Savior. Do not pass me by," but you are kidding yourself. How can he pass you by if he is already in you? What you need to be confessing is, "I can do all things through him who strengthens me" (Philippians 4:13).

Not only does God strengthen you, but as the next chapters will show, he is eager to speak his will to you.

3 || *What's Going On in There?*

I WOULD NEVER HAVE expected my mom to say something like this. She was a widow with five children, all of whom turned out to be ministers. She cooked for the pastors' conventions. She served as midwife for the neighborhood—without charging.

So it surprised me when I found her crying one day and she confided in me. I was already a minister, though still young.

"I don't know if I should tell you this, but I am a little upset," she said. "Everybody in the church feels spiritual things. One person feels electricity in her body. Another one feels a warm sensation and another feels a cold sensation. I never feel anything. Perhaps the Lord doesn't really love me."

We were members of a Pentecostal church. *Feeling* spiritual things was a big part of our unwritten code.

"Mom," I replied. "You're not feeling things because you are one that lives by faith."

I was not saying she was the only one truly saved, or the only one who loved God, but she related to God differently.

I have spent two chapters talking about how God dwells inside us. Not only did he place his Spirit in us, but as we will see, he operates largely through our own spirits. As captain of our conscience, God has a way to direct us that's better than the random jostling by the winds of feelings.

NEWNESS OF THE SPIRIT

We don't need to shy away from the idea of spirit— either the Holy Spirit or our own spirit. Scripture speaks of both. God wants us to understand them.

"But now we have been released from the Law, having died to that by which we were bound, so that we serve in newness of the Spirit and not in oldness of the letter" (Romans 7:6). That's encouraging—we serve God via his Spirit, and it's a new, fresh thing. And our spirit is involved, too. Paul said, "For God, whom I serve in my spirit..." (Romans 1:9).

Jesus was more explicit: "But an hour is coming, and now is, when the true worshipers shall worship the Father in spirit and truth; for such people the Father seeks to be his worshipers. God is spirit; and those who worship Him must worship in spirit and truth" (John 4:23-24).

True worship and service—both involve the spirit. When God created man, he did not forget to install a capacity for navigating in the spiritual realm. Many teachers have compared the three-part unity of God (Father, Son, and Holy Spirit) to a similar unity in man (body, soul, and spirit). The body, of course, possesses five senses and feels pain and pleasure quite tangibly. The soul encompasses our emotions and thought life. The innermost parts of our existence concern the spirit.

What we know as conscience—and even the secular world recognizes its existence—is another name for spirit. So if it helps you to understand the whole human package, consider the three parts as simply flesh, mind, and conscience.

RELATING TO A FATHER GOD

If your ankle is sprained, you limp, and everyone can read something about your physical condition. If you're upset with your spouse, a close friend will probably realize something is wrong even if you don't say anything about your frustration.

But nobody's antenna picks up a broadcast from your conscience unless God chooses to reveal something to them. Only God can penetrate through all the fuzzy stuff of our fleshly actions and soulish thought life to read our conscience all the time. He has a spirit-to-Spirit direct line.

But how can communication work between two parties who are so different? It seems as improbable as trying to hook up an old paper-tape calculator to a supercomputer.

For starters, God is perfect. He does not make mistakes, lose his temper, or need to repent for bad behavior. Yet we have Scripture intimating that he does such things. For example, Exodus 32:14 said God "repented" (KJV) or "changed His mind about the harm which He said He would do to His people."

I believe this is an example of God choosing to speak to us in our language for our benefit. In his perfection, God is changeless, somewhere above the vacillation that we experience in our imperfection.

When I am with young children, I speak their language: Da, da, da, duh, duh, flabba gooby womba. They speak back. We may not have 100 percent communication, but what we have flows. We communicate because I'm willing to speak their language.

So is God with us. He speaks with anger; he communicates with laughter. He speaks through your husband, your wife, your boss, your children, even your neighbor that you can't stand and who never goes to church. Let's not forget that the God who is Spirit chose to deliver his most important message through a being appearing in the flesh, Jesus.

Nevertheless, Jesus' physical days on earth are over. We cannot physically feel his touch, nor can we physically touch him. You may sing, "Taste and see that the Lord is good," but you never will literally because you can't touch God. The person standing next to you in the service may say, "I can feel his mighty hand" or "I hear the brush of angels' wings," but I'm afraid 99 percent of these feelings are physical sensations or emotions.

I'm not saying they're always false sensations. Sometimes just for fun, or to reveal himself more clearly, or because we are so childish in relation to God, he plugs in to one of our senses. We see a vision. We hear something audible. We feel something special as hands are laid on in prayer. God can reveal himself in any form he chooses because he is not limited.

I say all this not to rob your treasure chest of spiritual experiences. Rather, I want to help you clear away any clutter that keeps you from an unobstructed view of God. *God is a spirit; when he acts normally, he is not felt.* That's why there was no problem with my mom's lack of feeling. She was in love with a spirit God. He returned that love through her spirit, not her feelings. Her love was not conditional upon God activating her senses. Do you seek a normal relationship with God? Then walk by faith, not by sight or smell or touch or vision.

GOD'S FLASHLIGHT

Hebrews 12:9 says God is "the Father of spirits." "Spirits" refers not just to angels or the multi-headed creatures described in the book of Revelation. God is the Father of the spirit—the conscience—he placed in every person. He assigned to man and woman the role of being father and mother to physical bodies. But it is God who begets the spirit in each person.

This is why a person who rejects God often seems on the inside like a runaway or an orphan. The spirit is not in tune with its Father. This, too, explains why man and woman differ from animals. Because we have a spirit, we alone have the capacity to know God, to worship him, to speak to him, to serve him.

Proverbs 20:27 gives great insight as to how God uses our spirits, and it explains why I equate man's spirit with conscience: "The spirit of man is the lamp of the Lord, searching all the innermost parts of his being."

What does the lamp search for? He's not checking out whether you raise your hands in worship, or how loud you sing, or whether your eyes are open or closed. He's not looking for a log book of how many hours you've spent at church or how many days you've fasted. He's looking even deeper than your thought life, much of which is quite private. He wants to know everything about what's making you tick.

You may have been a Christian a long time, but if you are honest, you will admit that looking inside your life is like peering into the crawl space under an old house. Dark. Private. All sorts of forgotten junk, old treasures, creepy, crawling things, cobwebs, dusty and rotten things. God uses our conscience like a flashlight to begin exposing the dark corners of our inner life. He usually doesn't take a floodlight to turn the entire mess into a brightly lit stage. He just shines his light here, there, drawing our attention gradually.

As God interacts with our conscience, wonderful things happen, as we will see.

4 | *Should We or Shouldn't We?*

"**B**ROTHER, I think I need to divorce my husband. What do you think?" asks the woman.

"Do you believe that divorce is right in your case? Are you sure, what does your conscience say?" I ask.

"Oh, that I shouldn't."

"Then why are you coming to ask me what to do if you already know?"

The unspoken answer is that she is looking for a back door to escape from the course the Lord has already shown her. She wastes her time. Not because God cannot use me, as well as any other Christian, to give godly counsel, because he certainly can and does. But because I am not a judge, I cannot simply overrule the supreme court and its code of law, the Bible.

What supreme court? The conscience. As God speaks to us through our conscience, we receive, if we choose to, a stream of messages from him on matters big and small. God's judgments are infallible, but we are not. Because we remain subject to error and sin, our conscience and our response to it fall short. So as we explore the working of conscience, we'll also look at some of its shortcomings.

JUDGING THE MIDDLE GROUND

Many decisions fall outside black and white issues. That's one reason God gave us a conscience. "The faith which you have, have as your own conviction before God. Happy is he who does not condemn himself in what he approves" (Romans 14:22).

Should you eat that piece of cake? You may find lots of laws about diet in the Mosaic Law, and you'll see lots of numbers in the book of Numbers, but you won't find any clues there about your personal diet and your optimal waist size. You will, however, find more than a clue if you listen to your conscience. Unless you suffer from being overly scrupulous, if you're hearing something between yes and no, you're probably safest going with no. You won't die from sugar deprivation. And there's no time for a counseling session with your pastor, who has more important things to do anyway.

If you don't condemn yourself—that is, if your conscience doesn't—in approving that little indulgence, fine. This is the cake that the Lord has made; let us rejoice and be glad! Let's not fall into legalism, worrying about every small decision in our lives.

Eating, incidentally, prompted one of the Bible's primary passages about conscience, 1 Corinthians 8. The problem was whether to eat meat that had been sacrificed to idols. On the one hand, eating the food would not automatically condemn a Christian possessing knowledge that its dedication is meaningless to a servant of the true God. But there is a caution: "For if someone sees you, who have knowledge, dining in an idol's temple, will not his conscience, if he is weak, be strengthened to eat things sacrificed to idols?" (v. 10). Again, the court must speak to each person in a particular circumstance as to what would be sinful. Our conscience may allow us to do something as far as the effect on us, but if it indirectly creates problems in another's conscience, we may need to hold back.

THE CONSTRUCTIVE CONSCIENCE

The court also speaks in the positive sense about what we can do to please God. When I began my walk with God, he wanted to know if I would obey. All the time.

"I will," I said through clenched teeth. He could hear me screaming inside, "Owwww! This is going to hurt sometimes!"

Since then I've learned otherwise. Obeying God's voice through my conscience comes naturally. It's like learning to drive. At first you have to think about where the brake pedal is and how hard to push it. With time, the brakes and everything else about driving become automatic. So it is with God. He speaks. I respond. This vehicle he calls Juan Carlos Ortiz moves right along his path.

For example, I was having lunch with a pastor friend in an apartment he rented in Buenos Aires. My conscience was not invited, but it came anyway.

While we were eating, my conscience interrupted: "Do you have a house, Juan Carlos?"

"Yes. I have two," I replied.

"Your friend doesn't even have one."

Now sometimes you don't hear any more than that from your conscience. But that should be all you need. I began calling other friends to see about getting money for this brother to buy a house. It took me about a year to raise my share—by skipping restaurant meals, saving here and there. God did not cause a big pot of gold to drop out of heaven. Soon my friend was moving into his own house. Simple obedience to my conscience paid off.

SEARED, BUT NEVER DESTROYED

This matter of conscience is not just another installment in a long series of Christian teachings. Conscience is so basic that God has placed it in every person, Christian or otherwise. Its omnipresent operation explains why God has the right to judge *all* men, even those ignorant of the gospel:

> For when Gentiles who do not have the Law do instinctively the things of the Law, these, not having the Law, are a law to themselves, in that they show the work of the Law written in their hearts, their conscience bearing witness, and their thoughts alternately accusing or else defending them. **Romans 2:14-15**

This is not to say that those who don't know God always maintain a conscience as active as those whose spirits are tied in with God's. Ephesians 4:18-19 elaborates on the conscience of those bent on disregarding God—Gentiles

> being darkened in their understanding, excluded from the life of God, because of the ignorance that is in them, because of the hardness of their heart; and they, having become callous, have given themselves over to sensuality, for the practice of every kind of impurity with greediness.

Something callous has been worn out. A worn-out conscience no longer speaks. Or if it speaks, the voice is so smothered by other voices of self and flesh that it can no longer be distinguished. Paul refers to ungodly people "seared in their own conscience as with a branding iron" (1 Timothy 4:2). Sin has left its indelible mark on their conscience; in the process burning away something living.

The good news is that the lamp of the Lord, the spirit/conscience in man, never completely gets extinguished. As long as a sinner can find that glimmer and respond to it in repentance, it can be nurtured until it shines as brightly as the sun.

And this gives a new perspective on salvation. Hebrews 9:14 says "the blood of Christ" will "cleanse your conscience from dead works to serve the living God." Jesus can resuscitate the deadest of consciences. Not only does God renew our conscience, but he sends his Spirit to dwell in that conscience. As we have seen, God promised that the Spirit would guide us into all things, to teach us all truth. If conscience is the supreme court, the Spirit is the chief justice.

FALLIBLE FEELINGS

The Holy Spirit is infallible. We are not, and therefore our conscience is not. Partly this is because of how we feed the conscience: what we read, with whom we associate, our prayer life, our heart for God, the emphases of our particular denomination. Certain acts—watching a particular movie, or dancing—may offend one person's conscience, but not another's. But the point here is that no one's conscience functions at 100 percent.

God has given us two good checks on this built-in weakness. One is the counsel of mature Christians. You may have to make a decision on the spot whether to give money to a beggar. No big deal—you try to turn up the conscience volume and respond as you hear. But on bigger issues, say, moving to another country, you may need more time to decide and you probably need some wise counsel for verification. But don't go to people who are always *feeling* this and *feeling* that. Check with those who walk in proven faith, who relate to God as a Spirit, which he is.

The other balance, of course, is Scripture. You may not find verses that pertain to your exact decision, but the Spirit has a way of shining his light on certain themes or passages that cast a shadow over the bigger picture.

A clear, active conscience has a way of blending counsel, the Word of God, and circumstances in a way that yields a simple answer. But you have to want to listen, to be willing to wait, and to be prepared for surprises.

The answer may be very different from what you feel or like. Do you know what *I like?* One thing is the latest electronic gadget that shows up at the store—typewriter, computer, stereo components, whatever. For years I wanted a videocassette recorder. I had 60 videotapes of myself, so there was good reason to have one—to critique my teaching. Besides, all my friends had one.

It usually wasn't a matter of money. Three times I was in the store with enough money to buy one. I *felt* like buying one. I would have *liked* to buy one. But I *knew* I shouldn't. My conscience had another opinion: Wait. In one case, a week later, the money I had went to help buy a house for a widow. So God's purpose became clear, and I was so glad I had obeyed.

So be sure you do not approach this conscience dialogue with God only with concerns such as: What do I feel? What do I like? Such questions tend to take the matter out of the realm of the spirit and into that of the mind and body. That's not to say that you should totally disregard such emotions; God may use them as indicators to help guide you. If your mind is continually being transformed into the mind of Christ, the things you feel and like should increasingly fall in line with what God desires. Always ask yourself, "What do I know, what does my conscience tell me?"

Some Christians fear that God's will for us as revealed through the conscience is always going to be the finger-shaking, no-no-no kind. It's not. The same God who has pulled the reins on my gadget-buying has given me many good things. He created this vast world with its many pleasures. The same Spirit who speaks through our conscience has a fruit with nine virtues, all listed in the Bible. And guess what—one of them is joy!

At last I got my VCR. And when I did, God had already saved me money. When I first began looking at those machines, they cost $3,000. Now I paid well under $500.

I am getting ahead of myself. As you can see, the conscience plays a major part in self-control. And self-control is an essential element of Christ's indwelling presence. It provides a way for God to work through us.

5 | *Who's in Control of You?*

WE HAD A STUDENT from Mexico living with us in our California home. A Catholic, he was devoted to his church and to the Lord. He studied English at a school where there were four or five Muslim students. These were children of Arab sheiks, which meant they were children of money. They drove nice cars. They indulged their fleshly appetites.

Our Mexican friend also came from a wealthy family. The difference was that his parents were wise Christians. They had trained him well. (They also didn't give him a car!)

These good looking Arab boys were always bugging our boarder. "Jesus is of no value," they would say as they touted their religion. Since they outnumbered him, they could put him down easily.

Weekends were party time. The Arab boys would invite him to their festivities in a hotel, where they would sample all sorts of sin. He would go with them, but he didn't join in their sins.

Five months after they met, the Arabs were still on him: "Why don't you leave Jesus and come to our religion?"

"How can I leave Jesus?" the Mexican said. "My Jesus helped me not to sin, but your religion doesn't help you not to sin. Because when you go with the girls, I stay away. When you go to the porno movies, I stay home. Who gives me that self-control? Jesus."

They never talked religion again. I don't think those Arabs even wanted self-control. They probably knew that their religion would not approve those sins. But they lacked power. There is a simple reason: Only Jesus rose from the dead. He offered to place a divine spirit inside each believer that would grow and bear wonderful fruit, including self-control.

Yes, Jesus did.

As we deal with the fruit of the Spirit, I want to focus on self-control and its relationship to love. A greater understanding of self-control will do much to help us recognize and cultivate the new life that beats inside us.

THE SPIRIT MANIFEST

We have talked about men and women's greatest problem—evident in both Old and New Testament: our inability to obey God. Think about this for a moment. No one has to be trained to rebel. Any parent will testify what an inborn knack the youngest of children has for defying authority. And we saw how the Old Testament remedy for this problem consisted of a set of laws, with appropriate sanctions.

But then the prophet Ezekiel foretold a major change: "I will give you a new heart and put a new spirit within you; and I will remove the heart of stone from your flesh and give you a heart of flesh. And I will put My Spirit within you and cause you to walk in My statutes, and you will be careful to observe My ordinances" (Ezekiel 36:26-27).

Did Ezekiel say God would give us the Spirit so we could dance while we worship? So we could lift our hands while we sing? No, it was so that *we could obey God's laws.*

That's easy to say, you may be thinking. The reality is that sin comes just as easily as before, if not more easily. God knows this. And he revealed to us, through Paul, a glimpse of how the Spirit would help us in our quest for obedience: "The fruit of the Spirit is love, joy, peace, patience, kindness, goodness, faithfulness, gentleness, self-control; against such things there is no law" (Galatians 5:22-23).

Notice that there is no such thing as *fruits* of the Spirit. There is just one *fruit,* according to verse 22, but with nine wonderful elements. Something is amiss if you find yourself saying, "I really have a lot of love, but I just don't have any joy." The fruit of the Spirit is a package deal. When you buy a house, you don't purchase just certain rooms to live in. It's all or nothing. If the Holy Spirit is living in you, expect nothing less than these nine manifestations erupting all over.

FRUIT AND GIFTS

Sometimes the fruit of the Spirit is spoken of as the same thing as the gifts of the Spirit, such as wisdom, knowledge and speaking in tongues. But the fruit and gifts differ greatly.

What is fruit? It's the natural result of a healthy tree. You expect apples to pop out on the apple tree; you should expect the fruit mentioned in Galatians 5:22-23 to mark the Spirit-filled life.

What is a gift? For starters, you know it's not the natural produce of a tree, like a fruit is. Think of a Christmas tree. You hang ornaments on a tree and place gifts around it. All of a sudden, this plain tree becomes extraordinarily beautiful. Then Christmas comes, the gifts are removed, the ornaments packed away. The tree is consigned to the trash. It's only real value was in the gifts—those things placed there by an outside hand.

Now the Spirit gives to each one as he chooses. The Spirit may give the gift of prophecy or the gift of miracles. If the Spirit doesn't place it under your tree, you can't unwrap it.

You can't blame the apple tree for not producing gifts. You can blame it for failing to bear apples. Likewise, you can be excused for not raising the dead if God hasn't gifted you to do so. You cannot be excused from failing to exhibit love, joy, peace, and the other signs of the Spirit because these together are the expected fruit.

Consequently, when someone attempts to minister, you should be primarily concerned with the basics—the fruit—and not so much with the gifts. Gifts may mislead. Fruit does not. That's why Jesus issued this warning:

"Many will say to Me on that day, 'Lord, Lord, did we not prophesy in Your name, and in Your name cast out demons, and in Your name perform many miracles?' And then I will declare to them, 'I never knew you; depart from Me, you who practice lawlessness'" (Matthew 7:22-23).

That's also why Paul, in his beautiful passage on true love, puts gifts in the proper perspective: "Love never fails; but if there are gifts of prophecy, they will be done away; if there are tongues, they will cease; if there is knowledge, it will be done away" (1 Corinthians 13:8). He is not saying we must choose between fruit and gift, but rather to be sure the fruit is present before we marvel over the gifts.

LIVING BY CONVICTION

So if the fruit of the Spirit is present, you should be able to exercise self-control. Why do I single this one out? Because since God is so much closer than you think, the potential for self-control is greater than you may have ever realized. God resides within your very self.

If you have trouble with eating too much, you need to practice self-control. But who will be doing the controlling? If you just clench your teeth, make a huge bet with somebody, or cement your upper and lower molars together, you are the one calling the shots. And as you have probably experienced, the self-control that begins and ends with you too often fails. Even if your strategy works for a time, it often comes at the cost of an ulcer or some other manifestation of stress.

There is a higher way.

First, let's look at the opposite of a self-controlled person. This is a person who is sensual. He or she can be recognized by a craving for sex, food, alcohol or drugs—four common sensual delights to which many people surrender. Yet on a broader scale, we are still talking about the whole realm of feelings—fleshly feelings, emotional feelings, even spiritual feelings—that could also qualify as sensual.

I've said that the opposite of living by feelings is living by obedience to the conscience, but for the time being, let's phrase it differently. Living by *convictions* is the direct opposite of living by sensuality. A conviction is something you *believe*. Sometimes you may not feel love for your spouse, but if you have a conviction that your marriage is an eternal covenant before God, and that you are bound to love your spouse, you will not be distracted from your commitment by your feelings. Of course, time may prove your feelings were wrong. But the person of conviction does not need to reckon with feelings before acting.

I am not saying that feelings are bad or that they will always lead us astray. God gave us the ability to feel and this ability is part of our nature. God can work through our feelings. But our feelings are not to control us. We shouldn't ignore them or repress them or fear them, but neither should we bow down and worship them.

Do you believe exercise is good for your health? Do you believe it strongly enough to have formed a conviction about it? If so, you will pull your body out of bed in the morning, put on your jogging suit and run, even if you *feel* like you need more sleep, or you know that when you get outside you will *feel* cold. If your belief remains up there in the realm of "facts I know to be true" but not as deep as "something I will live by," there will be constant war. Sometimes the fact will win, sometimes the flesh will win.

The Holy Spirit is the author of our most important convictions. He speaks them to us in our spirits, and we can choose to embrace them. So *to walk in the Spirit is to walk by conviction*. To exercise self-control is to decide I will live as I know I should, not as I feel I would like to.

Of course, that's easier said than done.

NO FOOTHOLD FOR SATAN

Suppose you have trouble with anger. You get so angry that your words become like hornets stinging every member of your family. Is anger a sin? Ephesians 4:26 says, "Be angry, and yet do not sin; do not let the sun go down on your anger." So it's not a sin to get angry. How about eating—is it a sin to eat? To rest? To work? To sleep? To have sex? No. These natural functions are not sinful, provided we can control them and that they are done in the right context and not to excess.

Paul said the same thing: "All things are lawful for me, but not all things are profitable. All things are lawful for me, but I will not be mastered by anything" (1 Corinthians 6:12). Does anything master you? For some people, sleeping controls them, or sex controls them. Even seemingly little things—cigarettes, chocolate, coffee—can control you. Now these things may not seem to affect other areas of your life, but if you can't say no to them, if they ring the bell every day and your body comes panting, crouched at their feet, guess who's in control?

For many of these things, the key is the extent of involvement. With anger, for example, the Ephesians passage actually says "be angry." So there is obviously a place for anger. We should be angry when we see injustice or when our children act obstinately or when another human being is degraded. And we are human. Everyone's frail temperament has its limits.

But the rest of the Scripture about anger says not to sin, and furthermore to deal with that anger before the sun sets. Get angry and set the timer. As soon as you can, call that person who's pumped up your blood pressure. "Listen, brother, I forgive you" or "Sister, it was my fault to begin with." Do whatever is necessary. This is self-control—having a partnership with God's Spirit, not allowing yourself to be controlled by anger.

The verse following the anger passage warns: "Do not give the devil an opportunity," or in another translation, "a foothold" (Ephesians 4:27). Satan gains his foothold when we refuse to set the timer. I'm angry with you, my co-worker, so I show up at work the next morning and refuse to say hello. I leave to go home, further angered that you have not apologized, and I do not say goodbye. The devil has established his foothold and starts building it into a huge wall.

A moment's anger gets transformed into lasting resentment. Consider for a moment that *resent* has Latin roots made of two parts: *sent*, meaning feel, and *re*, meaning again. Resenting someone or something involves feeling the anger over and over. Give Satan the least opportunity, and he'll work to make sure we keep replaying our anger.

Much better to never cede control, but to act from conviction with Spirit-led self-control.

Even emotions with less sinful potential than anger are subject to this same principle. Suppose a loved one dies. If you are sad, this is good and natural. But if you fail to set the timer, problems arise. Satan grabs another foothold. Prolonged sadness may turn to depression. If you have lost a spouse, you may start praying, "Lord, I don't want to live any longer. Take me to heaven." You begin entertaining suicidal thoughts. You have forfeited your self-control. You may not get suicidal, but perhaps you maintain the funereal atmosphere—always crying, feeling sorry for yourself, making it hard for old friends to be around you. After a while, there will be fewer and fewer of those friends who bother to try.

What is the proper amount of grieving? I cannot say. That is why this aspect of self-control must be one of Spirit-to-spirit, of well-formed convictions, of listening to one's conscience.

At some point eating becomes gluttony, but we cannot escape the need to eat. Many Christians are against alcohol, and that is OK if that's their conviction. Yet in Argentina, we drink a glass of wine at the table. In Germany, after a service, the pastor may take you to a bar for a beer. But unquestionably, drunkenness is a sin. Godly self-control must help us draw the line between freedom and sinful excess.

I say all this not as some pep talk to help you conquer bad habits and to temper extreme lifestyles, but to highlight the potential for victory that lies within you. The normal Christian life bears the fruit of the Spirit, and that includes self-control. The kind of self-control God made possible for us is a self controlled by the one all-knowing captain, one who makes no mistakes in his decisions. Knowing that you have this power within, use it. Give Satan no opportunity to sink his roots into your life.

6 | Forgiveness and Peace

Have you ever lost something small? You look for it everywhere—under furniture, in pockets, in drawers—but it's nowhere. Finally you get desperate enough to search that one last place where maybe, just maybe, it has ended up.

So you go out to the garbage can and start rooting around. It's hard to avoid touching the slimy old leftovers and rotting chicken bones with sauce on them. The smell, especially if it's summer, practically drives you away before you start.

That's what it's like when we constantly think about someone's sins or offenses. We dive into the emotional/ spiritual garbage can and pick through the things that were disposed of, that were supposed to stay disposed of, and we experience them in all their glorious noxiousness.

Yuk!

We have talked about the importance of self-control, and its great potential because of him who is so close. The area of forgiveness presents a great challenge for self-control and Spirit-control to rule together in our lives. Without maintaining a state of forgiveness, we trade the sweet smell of peace that is rightfully ours because Christ lives within us, for a fitful romp in the garbage. And without that peace—with God and with others—we cannot fully enter into the kind of prayer life that we will be discussing in later chapters.

A TWO-WAY STREET

If the New Testament makes one thing clear about forgiveness, it's that forgiveness is a two-level affair. God expects us to forgive because he forgives us. This is reflected in the Lord's Prayer: "And forgive us our debts, as we also have forgiven our debtors" (Matthew 6:12). Jesus emphasized the principle immediately after giving his disciples the Lord's Prayer: "For if you forgive men for their transgressions, your heavenly Father will also forgive you. But if you do not forgive men, then your Father will not forgive your transgressions" (Matthew 6:14-15).

Some people say the Lord's Prayer is the curse of the Church. Because we are so prone to fall short in forgiving others, we automatically invite God to be intolerant of our sins.

That's why Jesus gave the parable of the steward who could not repay the huge debt he owed his master (Matthew 18). The steward received forgiveness from his debt, then turned around and abused someone who owed him a trifling amount and had him thrown into prison. When the master heard about this, he was steamed. He had the steward turned over to the torturers until he repaid every last cent. The lesson for us is that if God can forgive us so much—all our past and future offenses—should we not forgive others for their much more limited offenses toward us?

"Oh, but pastor, you don't know," I have heard so many times. "Carol has said this and this about me. And this was after I loaned her money to fix her car. I try to be nice to her, but every time she treats me...." Do you have a Carol in your life? Most of us have at least one person like that. So God included this little challenge in the Bible: "Then Peter came and said to Him, 'Lord, how often shall my brother sin against me and I forgive him? Up to seven times?' Jesus said to him, 'I do not say to you, up to seven times, but up to seventy times seven'" (Matthew 18:21-22).

TAKE OUT THE GARBAGE

Just as God does not want us digging through our spiritual garbage can, he, too, is not too keen on rummaging through garbage. Psalm 103:12 describes God's waste removal mission statement: "As far as the east is from the west, so far has He removed our transgressions from us." Now if God had said from the north and the south, you could imagine the North Pole and the South Pole. Though they're far apart, their distance can be measured. But if you get in an airplane and fly east or west, you never get to the east or the west. You just keep going.

So it is with our sins. If we fail to confess them, they can be as close as the space between our ears. If we confess them to God, he lets them pass on through to the eternal journey eastward or westward.

Let's be real, though. You may forgive someone else, and still have difficulty *forgetting* the trespass in the way God would. But forgiveness doesn't require that we forget a wrong done to us. If your grandfather physically abused you as a child, it may not be safe or possible for you to forget the abuse. But forgiveness means you do not hold a judgment in your heart against someone. You do not live in hope that they will suffer for the wrong done to you. You release them to God and let him decide the outcome, and you even pray that God will bless them. If you can forget, fine, but if not, that doesn't mean you haven't forgiven.

One clear step you can take is to decide that you will not dwell forever on the wrong done to you. You may need to talk it through with a trusted friend or counselor, but you will not let yourself become obsessed by how terribly you were treated. To do so is to be rooting around in the garbage. And you will begin to stink as a result. You will take on the aroma of the environment in which you place yourself.

A woman in my church hated her daughter-in-law. Every week this woman told me new stories. One day I said, "Stop it! My ear is not a garbage can." That's the other problem. Those who enjoy—or even merely tolerate—hearing someone's old grievances are inadvertently becoming garbage receptacles themselves.

Don't let yourself become contaminated with others'

leftovers. If someone comes to unload a problem on you, see if you can give wise counsel. If you sense that the person doesn't want help, say, "Let's go and tell this to the person involved, and then we can settle it for good."

Garbage is real. You can't ignore it for long. But you must find the best way to dispose of it, quickly and for good. There's no point in passing it around endlessly.

DON'T KEEP WAITING

When an offense takes place, sometimes the resolution proceeds according to the textbook. The person who offended you comes to you, expresses sorrow, asks forgiveness, and shows a willingness to make restitution. You suggest that the offender correct previous statements made about you to another person, and this is done. Wouldn't it be great if it always happened like this?

But it rarely does. Too often, the people who hurt us refuse to admit it. As the weeks following an offense turn into months, and then years, you can choose to forgive or not forgive. If you make forgiveness conditional on their repentance, you are not really forgiving.

If you forgive with a condition, saying, "I will forgive you, if you say this and repay that," that is forgiveness with a mortgage. Because if the indebted person falls short, you repossess what you had given—your forgiveness. The one who suffers is you, not the other person, because you are the one remaining in bondage, waiting for the completion of conditions. Yet if the offender has truly repented, he or she is free of guilt. You can be just as free if you forgive regardless of what the other person does. You've heard the expression "Get a life"? That's what forgiveness does. It forces us to take personal responsibility to take our lives out of neutral and put them back in gear.

Sometimes the issue gets clouded. Once I needed to forgive other people because they thought they were in the right and I was wrong, but I knew differently. They still think that way. Maybe they were right and I was wrong. Who knows? But the only way to clarify such problems is to forgive *regardless* of the verdict, since neither you nor I will ever have an authoritative judgment this side of heaven.

Another temptation in these tangled problems is to confuse forgiveness with clarification. I once called two people to try and clarify a problem among us. It only made things worse!

That's why unilateral forgiveness—no clarification, no excuses, no conditions—is the highest way. Unilateral means: *from one side.* The other person may not even know he or she has done something that needs to be forgiven. That's OK. It is the Holy Spirit's job to convict the person, not yours. You do your part and forgive.

This is often hard, but it is the Bible's way. Remember the lame man let down to Jesus through the hole in the roof? Jesus said, "Your sins are forgiven." The man had not asked for forgiveness, but he got it, and was healed, too. The adulterous woman whom the Pharisees brought before Jesus did not know what to expect, except the flying stones called for in the Old Testament. Yet Jesus said, "I forgive you. Go and sin no more." That was unilateral forgiveness.

The greatest example we have is the one Jesus gave on

the cross. None of the soldiers or Jewish priests came begging Jesus for forgiveness. They did not entreat him to intercede on their behalf before the Father. Yet Jesus, after suffering excruciating pain and being near death, could utter, "Father, forgive them."

The ability to issue unilateral forgiveness is evidence that Jesus was more than just a nice guy. He had power. Because he lives in us, we have that power, too.

7 | *The Power in Forgiveness*

A THIEF KILLED the brother of a friend of mine, a powerful minister. All my friend's church background, all his spiritual experience, had not prepared him for the unshakable bitterness that followed his brother's murder.

This pastor prayed about it. He kept praying. After three years of praying, he still did not have victory over grief and over his resentment toward the killer.

So finally he went to the prison and asked to see this man. The jail officials knew the pastor, and denied him permission, figuring he was seeking revenge. But he kept asking, and at last the prison officials gave in.

"I've come to tell you that I forgive you. That I love you," said my friend. "And if you allow me, I will come to visit you every week and pray with you."

That forgiveness and love helped bring this prisoner to

the Lord. He is serving a life sentence, but he is using the rest of his life to conduct a prison ministry and he is bearing fruit for God.

Is that not amazing? Forgiveness is more than just doing the right thing. It is more than the step you take to clear your bitterness or the offender's conscience. *Forgiveness involves power.* There is power in forgiveness because true forgiveness draws upon the compassion, the love, and the strength of Jesus, who lives within us. It produces the kind of peace that God alone can give.

POWER TO RELEASE

Jesus linked peace, the Holy Spirit, power and forgiveness: "'Peace be with you; as the Father has sent Me, I also send you.' And when He had said this, He breathed on them, and said to them, 'Receive the Holy Spirit. If you forgive the sins of any, their sins have been forgiven them; if you retain the sins of any, they have been retained'" (John 20:21-23).

When we think of the Holy Spirit's manifestations in our lives, we probably think of guidance and special promptings. If we think big, we envision healings and other miracles. But what about forgiveness? This is what Jesus emphasized when he spoke of the Spirit. This is no accident. Because forgiveness is often impossible from a human standpoint, we *need* God's power, made available through the Helper, the Spirit, to forgive.

God gives us the power to release people from their indebtedness to us. They owe us, we think, because they've wronged us. But many of the people who we think owe us don't even acknowledge their debt. Maybe they don't understand it, or refuse to acknowledge it. It doesn't matter what *their* reason is because God gives *you* the power to release them. Don't carry that corpse of a spoiled relationship around on your shoulder indefinitely. Unilateral forgiveness frees you and in the process gives you power to live for Christ, to pour your energies into something constructive.

This is the pattern Jesus set, as Paul explained: "But God demonstrates His own love toward us, in that while we were yet sinners, Christ died for us" (Romans 5:8). God's offer of forgiveness precedes our repentance. The prodigal son's father did the same, forgiving him before he ever returned home. The prodigal's dad did not demand a long apology and numerous promises from his son never to disgrace his family again. No, he ran out to meet his son, embraced him, forgave him, and put on a big party to celebrate his son's return.

Whenever there is a need for forgiveness, a sort of evil, or demonic spiritual bond can form. Two people are bound together in an unhealthy way. If you have been offended and you opt for unilateral forgiveness instead of waiting for the other person to come crawling to your feet, you break that chain. You cut Satan's power in that situation. By your *one* act, *both* parties begin to change. Instead of stagnating, the relationship and the individuals can resume growing.

Mary Welch, in her book *The Golden Key*, tells about a woman who was the victim of so much false slander that her church finally excommunicated her. Since she lived in a small town, that made matters worse—everyone knew about her situation and everyone in the church avoided her. So she hated the pastor, the elders, everyone in the church. For seven years, she stayed mostly in her home, wishing that God would punish the church. She was so lonely that she thought, "If they would just ask forgiveness, I would forgive them. But if they won't, I won't forgive them."

So while she waited, she suffered. She ruined herself emotionally. Finally, she got out a map of the city and prayed over it, releasing everyone involved in the slanderous attack, asking God to bless them. When she returned to church, everyone received her. They loved her. *Nobody asked her forgiveness, and she did not mention that she had forgiven them.* But things began to change for the better. Unfortunately, it took her seven years to find the way out of an emotional prison sentence that she was not entirely responsible for. But that's the power God has granted us in forgiveness—we do not have to depend on insensitive, capricious people to put an end to wrong. We have the power of Christ, the prime forgiver, to set the captives, even Christian captives, free.

FALLING SHORT IN FORGIVENESS

Just as forgiveness is a positive source of power and healing, the lack of forgiveness is not just a neutral circumstance, but a negative one that can bring with it sickness and other problems. You can't put a situation needing forgiveness on the back burner and expect it to fade away.

Failure to forgive results in anger, resentment, complaining, depression, and all sorts of emotional disturbances. It even affects things much bigger than your one troublesome relationship. Look at the Middle East, where the Jews and Arabs appear to be incapable of forgiving each other. They have a laundry list hundreds of years old: unprovoked attacks, maiming and killing of innocent people, the taking of property, and so on. No question that these things are hard to forgive. But can peace ever come to this region without forgiveness? No way. There may be moments of peace, but no major step forward will come without that attitude of unilateral forgiveness from both sides.

Even within the church, forgiveness is a major stumbling block. As Paul said, "Let all bitterness and wrath and anger and clamor and slander be put away from you, along with all malice. And be kind to one another, tenderhearted, forgiving each other, just as God in Christ also has forgiven you" (Ephesians 4:31-32). The gates of hell cannot prevail against the church, but lack of forgiveness can sure throw up a few roadblocks.

A woman once came to the elders in our church to do something about her husband, who I believe truly was a rascal.

"Dear brothers, I don't want you to misunderstand me. I want to divorce him, but I forgive him. The only thing I ask is that he never see me or the children again. I don't want him ever to set foot in our house."

I said, "If this is what you demand when you forgive him, what would you demand if you did not forgive him?" I wasn't saying she was wrong to feel as she did; I wasn't saying that the husband didn't deserve this; he did. And in cases where a man is inflicting serious physical and mental abuse on his wife or children, separation is essential.

But I could not agree with her version of forgiveness. She wanted him to pay for his sins by isolating him from his family. Suppose you confess a sin to God, asking forgiveness. He responds, "Hey, no problem, I forgive you. But you know, that last sin put you over your lifetime limit. You're going to hell when you die." This is not the kind of forgiveness our God offers us.

When I challenged this woman, she began to weep.

"Don't cry," I said. "I think I understand. And God understands. But be honest—tell God you can't really forgive your husband now. God will understand."

Forgiveness is not easy, so let's not pretend that it is. It's only for committed Christians bent on doing God's will, those serious about obeying God, who commanded us to forgive.

HANDLING REPENTANCE

I have been talking about problems often stemming from situations where the offender does not ask forgiveness. But other problems can arise when someone repents of sin. Here are two points to consider, especially for leaders.

We have to be careful that we come not against the sinner but against the sin. Suppose Satan entices a Christian woman to sin. My initial tendency may be to come against Satan *and* the woman. But who is the real enemy? Satan is. I should join with the woman and together with her come against Satan, against the sin, in prayer, in working out forgiveness. It's been said that Satan never kills a Christian; he just hurts her and other Christians finish her off.

How true it is that the church is the only army that shoots its wounded.

Part of this care for the sinner involves confidentiality. Whether you are in leadership or not, you must prove yourself absolutely trustworthy about not revealing others' sins. The passage of time, or changing circumstances, do not suddenly give us a green light to reveal matters told in confidence.

The second point is that *when you are hearing someone's confession, let the person speak, then ask them questions, and do not communicate forgiveness in a hurry.* Why the caution? Sometimes a confession is not honest. Beware of someone who tries to spread the blame around.

"Brother Ortiz, I have to confess that I committed adultery. But my wife is the problem because she always ignores me. She treats me like a dog. And then this other woman was always so kind...." This man is blaming everyone but himself. Others may share some blame, but their share does not diminish his guilt.

In such a case, I tell the person, "Go home and pray about this some more. I don't think you are confessing properly. Come back tomorrow and we'll talk."

When I see that a person has truly repented, that he hates his sins like God hates them, that he understands the stain he has brought on the body of Christ and the consequences that have affected certain people, then I express forgiveness. I don't pass out forgiveness like Christmas cards.

A member of my staff in Argentina began a church in another city and was enjoying great success. Then one day he fell into a horrible sin.

He said to me, "Juan Carlos, I know I am wrong," my

friend confessed to me amid tears. "I am guilty 100 percent. I place myself in your hands. If you tell me to throw myself in the river tied to a big stone, I will do it. If you tell me to go to Brazil or Australia, I'll leave. You tell me what you want."

So I said that according to our rules, I would remove him from his ministry. I told him his salary would be cut and I was not sure if he would preach again.

I went to my office to pray. My conscience said to me, "How easily you did that. When he was doing well, you shared his glory. Now that he is doing badly, you don't want to share the blame. You cut him off. Maybe he will die of sadness and depression, but you have saved your own life. The holy Juan Carlos Ortiz doesn't allow any sin in his church. Juan Carlos, the truth is that his failure is your failure, just as his success was your success. He is part of you."

So I told my friend, "Forgive me. I haven't really forgiven you. Because if I had, I would have treated you differently. I wouldn't make you pay first. You will have your full salary, for you will need it more today than ever before since you must stop preaching while you deal with the consequences of this sin."

"Pastor, that is crazy," he said. "Don't you know what other people will say about you and about our church?"

I said, "You should have thought about that before you sinned. Now you will see how much we will pay for your sins. But because we love you and you are one of us, we will suffer the blame together."

And we did. The criticism and gossip were worse than any discipline I could have invented. My friend even asked me to release him, so he could go to another country.

"No, sir," I said. "You must stay and learn that what you have done is no trivial thing. Restitution will take time."

He learned—and we all learned—what it meant for Jesus to identify with our sins. Jesus laid down his life for the brethren and we have to do the same. Jesus received the lashes that we deserved, and sometimes we have to receive some of the lashes meant for our brother or sister in Christ.

Forgiveness is not easy. The most natural thing is to strike back when someone hits you. That requires no power, only reflex. The real need for a power infusion, for Spirit-aided self-control, comes when we must refrain from hitting back. That is what Christian maturity calls us to do.

We can do all things—even forgive the most unforgivable situation—through Christ who strengthens us. When we stand cleansed of our sins, free of any unresolved problems with others, how much better prepared we are to cultivate the kind of prayer life God invites us to have.

8 | *Pray without Deceasing*

Do you have prayer chains in your church? You know, those lists where you sign up to pray every night from 7 to 8, or even at some dark hour that means crawling out from your warm bed when sane people are visiting dreamland. The unwritten rule in churches I've been in was that if you didn't sign, you weren't spiritual.

So I would sign. The hour would come, and I would pray. After a while, I would sneak a look at my watch. Only five minutes gone! Fifty-five more to go!

Why is prayer like this? Suppose your boyfriend or girl-friend tells you, fifteen minutes into a date, "Oh, no, still three hours to be with you." You might wonder why your partner even bothered to spend time with you. I think God often wonders the same thing about his children who approach him in prayer.

Admit it—what is the least attended meeting in church? The prayer meeting. You can even catch preachers saying, "Well, it's *only* a prayer meeting."

For the next few chapters I am going to critique our traditional approach to prayer. Actually, I have nothing against prayer. But I want to dispel some misconceptions about the way we go about prayer.

Prayer is one of God's greatest gifts to us. The possibility of prayer reminds us that we have access to God. How incredible! This access cost the sacrifice of Christ. He suffered, and with his blood paved a highway straight to the throne of our Father, a Father who had been distant up to that point. Prayer is the supersonic vehicle by which we travel to God.

The road is open to all. You may be a mature Christian adult or a seven-year-old. You may be a deaf mute. You may have committed the kinds of sins that give God every right to refuse to return your phone calls. But the thing common to us all is that God will listen. You don't have to be in church. You don't have to be the most faithful link in a prayer chain. You don't have to practice a daily devotion. God will listen anytime, anywhere. What a gift!

And because prayer is a gift from on high, we are obliged to be good stewards of it. We must improve it and cultivate it. Otherwise, we will experience continual frustration in our walk with God.

IS PRAYER AN ACTIVITY OR WAY OF LIFE?

When God created two-legged creatures capable of prayer, I imagine he thought, "Well, these people will sure be excited to communicate with their Creator. What an opportunity—to talk with God!" Instead, we have made prayer into the opposite of what God intended. It's as if someone gave you shoes and you used them for flower pots while your bare feet became cold and bloody.

Mishandling prayer is not a new problem. Even the early church needed a warning: "You ask and do not receive, because you ask with wrong motives, so that you may spend it on your pleasures" (James 4:3). Other Scripture versions say "you ask amiss" or "from wrong purpose and evil, selfish motives."

Can prayer to the one true God be selfish and evil? Even from nice Christians with good intentions? Yes, this happens—more than you think. Because Scripture indicates that prayer can be misdirected, that it can even be completely at odds with God's purposes, I want to address some major problem areas. The rest of this chapter will explore the first problem: when prayer becomes an activity, not a way of life.

Suppose you decide, "I will pray every morning from 6 to 6:30." That's an activity. It may be a good activity if it helps you establish a relationship with God that was absent due to your lack of discipline. But if that's the sum total of your fellowship with God, you're missing the point. Men, would your wives be content if you scheduled a half-hour block of conversation every day, but you ignored them the rest of the time?

Prayer is like that because prayer is life. It is life with another person who wishes to be intimate with us; it is life with one who is our very life source. Is Jesus Christ just a transient who needs a peanut butter sandwich from you whenever he passes your way? No. He lives in you all the time. The least you can do is to talk with him all the time.

We have all read, "Pray without ceasing" (1 Thessalonians 5:17). And most of us have figured, well, that's not quite possible, so it must mean, "Pray a lot." Sorry, but "without ceasing" means without ceasing, non-stop. This, too, reminds us that prayer is not an activity, but a *flow*. Suppose you and I are going on a long car trip. I tell you, "I'll be glad to talk with you from 6 to 6:30 on our trip. The rest of the time, my mind will be elsewhere, so you had better pay attention and mention anything important to me during that half hour."

Silly, isn't it? We would never make communication with a friend seem like a sacrifice. Yet too often we let God know our prayer is a sacrifice of our precious time and effort. Is breathing a sacrifice? No. We can breathe without even thinking about it. In fact, we can't stop breathing except for a matter of seconds. It's even pleasurable, in a sense.

We sing, "He walks with me and he talks with me as we go the narrow way." That's the way it should be. Walking and talking with God, just like breathing, should not tire you. Activities will wear you out. *Life* won't.

That's why, for example, when a new year rolls around, we should not be saying, "I will start praying this year." We should never be starting and stopping prayer. We should be praying without ceasing. What is another name for that which never ceases? Life. If you cease breathing, you *decease*. Cease praying, you begin to die spiritually. Prayer is a kind of spiritual breathing.

THE SPIRIT-LED WALK

Many people think the idea of walking in the Holy Spirit is too deep. But it's not deep. It's not even difficult.

To walk in the Spirit is to be continually conscious that Christ is within you.

I stress *continually*. How often we become conscious of Christ's presence in the worship service. "I really felt God's presence in that meeting," someone will say. "The Lord was really there today."

Well, where was he before you showed up? Was he hanging from the rafters, waiting for your loud songs to wake him up? No, we bring Christ with us because we live with him. It's not unusual to sense his presence more easily in a gathering of believers, or to feel him in a special way occasionally. But we are mistaken if we regard him as a celebrity who makes special appearances only at events with sufficient spiritual voltage. As soon as we develop that mentality, we're linking God with activities. Jesus did not come to bring us activities; he came to bring us life, abundant life, an ongoing experience.

Suppose I go to your house Monday morning. I knock on the door and nobody answers. I knock again. Nothing.

"Anybody home?" I yell. No response. But I hear noise inside, so I say, "Hello! How are you?"

You still don't answer, so I let myself in. I follow you to the kitchen, the bathroom and the bedroom, saying, "I want to talk to you." I trail you to the supermarket, to your job, but you never answer me. This goes on all of Monday, Tuesday, the whole week.

Sunday morning comes, and you are all smiles at the service. You are practically in song as you greet me, "Brother Ortiz, Brother Ortiz, Alleluia!"

"Hush," I say. "I was in your house all week. I followed you everywhere. But you never acknowledged my presence."

Christ is continually with us. To live in the Spirit is to

be continually communing with him. Why wait for the next prayer meeting when he's already meeting you where you are?

The two disciples walking to Emmaus (Luke 24) were talking about Christ, and once he appeared, they were literally walking with him. But they still were not aware of his presence. When they finally rested at the village and Jesus had communion with them, their eyes were opened. It was Jesus! Now this was something to trumpet—a private meal with the risen Savior. They hustled back to Jerusalem to blab to the apostles.

Too often, we are like the two disciples. We're strolling around with the King of Kings, close enough to touch him, but we foolishly wait for some glorious communion or worship service before we allow the eyes of our hearts to be opened. Because Christ is with us constantly, we should join fully in his fellowship along every step of the dusty road.

WE NEED INTIMACY WITH GOD

Does a healthy, continual conversation with the Lord mean that you never need to pause and be alone with him? Don't get me wrong. I am not saying that those of you with a daily quiet time should stop this sort of practice or activity. Quite the opposite.

I talk with my wife continually when I am home, and frequently by telephone when I am traveling. Yet sometimes I say, "Let's go get coffee somewhere, away from the telephone, away from the kids, so we can talk about how we are going to pay for our son to go to college."

Other times I suggest we go away for two or three days to a hotel to be alone and rest, to enjoy one another's presence.

Having these special times does not mean I can skip everyday communication, and vice versa. Both are parts of our relationship. When I first came to know Martha, we had ordinary conversation, some of it in a group setting. But as the relationship became more serious, we needed to have more intimate talks together. Likewise, the more we become friends with Christ, the more we want to be alone with him. It's not duty, it's not coercion, it's not legalism. It's not a heavy, boring intrusion on an otherwise exciting day. It's a pleasure to talk with God alone, without interruptions.

Sometimes I'm talking with God while driving on a long trip, and I sense he wants my complete attention. I say, "Wait a minute. Let's talk this over more thoroughly." So I stop the car, and my mind and spirit are completely free to finish our discussion. Once I see what the Lord wanted to show me, I crank up and I'm back on my way.

Taking special times to pray is a good thing, but it is nothing more than an *activity* if that is our only communication with God. A personal prayer session should come as a corollary, a consequence of our continual prayer life and our desire to be with God in a more intimate way. A regular time alone with him is certainly better than no conversation at all, or than dependence on an emotional fix every Sunday morning. But this daily rendezvous will never become all that it should be unless we are cultivating a relationship that makes us yearn to be with God all the time.

9 | *Is God Hard of Hearing?*

WHEN I RETURN HOME from a trip, my wife always picks me up at the airport. I have driven between home and the airport so many times that I could do it with my eyes closed.

Nevertheless, she says things like, "Turn right at the next corner." "Now stick to the left because you'll have to make a left turn."

I already know this. But that doesn't matter. Do you know why I don't complain about all this unnecessary instruction? Because I know that for some reason, Martha needs it for herself. I don't need the directions, but she needs to verbalize them.

In the spiritual—or perhaps I should say religious—realm, we often say and do things because *we* need to, not because God needs it. If we continue to grow spiritually, we will eventually shed some of these habits.

I am thinking about the next problem with prayer I want to address: *Prayer does not have to be repeated.* God, of course, is all-patient and he understands our motives, so there is nothing really bad about repeating prayers to God. But God is not deaf. He is not retarded. He hears us the first time.

I bring this to you not as teaching unequivocal gospel truth, but to expose you to an aspect of prayer you may never have considered. Please bear with me. See if God might show you a more effective way to pray.

WAKE UP, LORD!

Before looking specifically at prayer repetition, consider our typical attitude in prayer. We often begin with the presupposition that God is far away: "LORD! HEAR OUR PRAYER!" We equate prayer volume with sincerity of heart. "STRETCH FORTH THY HAND! MOVE! HEAL! SAVE!" And so on. Are you imagining that hand extending from 500 trillion light-years away in space, or from within you and from within your fellow believers?

Remember John the Baptist: "The kingdom of heaven *is at hand.*" Remember Pentecost: The promised deposit of the Holy Spirit was fulfilled. Christ in us, the hope of glory, has not gone on retreat. He remains Emmanuel, *God with us.*

I'm not railing against shouting or crying in prayer or worship. If it helps you, fine. But God doesn't need it. And if you do make a practice of running your prayers through a loudspeaker, be careful not to deceive yourself into thinking that the extra volume is necessary to reach a

God who has drifted farther away.

It's this same attitude that leads us into thinking we need to say prayers over and over again. We may use many different words that say the same thing. We try to make the same petition more eloquently than the sister who just prayed. We believe that God will finally understand, or give in, if we say the same prayer every day for a month, or for years.

We treat God like a slot machine. You put a coin in the machine, pull the handle, and see if you score. If you do, you can quit. If you don't, you'll probably try again and again, as long as your change holds out, waiting for the Big Payoff. So we make our prayers like coins. Chinggg, brrr. Chinggg, brrr. Over and over.

I can't help but wonder if repeating prayers doesn't often reveal a sense of doubt. Are you operating on forty percent faith, figuring that God hears maybe forty percent of your prayers, so you better turn loose a shotgun blast to cover that other sixty percent? James warned about mixing petitions with doubting: "Let him ask in faith without any doubting, for the one who doubts is like the surf of the sea driven and tossed by the wind. For let not that man expect that he will receive anything from the Lord" (James 1:6-7).

Many of us have used a prayer list. You go through it in the morning and you feel better. Miss it, and you feel a little guilty. Some days you are so spiritual that you repeat it in the afternoon, and you really feel like you've racked up a few extra points.

Now God is hearing these prayers. But be honest— does God want you in a *religion* or a *relationship*? If we are in a relationship, we talk often, more than once a day, and it's different each time. Imagine carrying on the same conversation with your spouse *every day*. You might change a word or two, but the content is the same. It would quickly become pointless for both of you.

Again, I don't condemn anyone for repeating prayers. God knows he created us with feelings, with a psychological makeup that craves familiarity and tradition. Look at our church meetings. There are certain things we expect and we almost deem them holy (though we'd never admit it)—the organ, the choir dressed in robes, the processional. These add up to a certain package that gives us a psychological picture of God's holiness, of how we might best worship him.

Religious trappings and habits can be like spices. I can eat pasta with or without basil, oregano, and garlic. But because God gave me taste, it's natural that I'd rather let the noodles pass through my mouth with some tantalizing spices. Yet the substance remains the same. It fills my belly no more, no less. It offers the same amount of nutrition. We may need to repeat our requests, but God doesn't need to have us repeat them.

REPETITION IN SCRIPTURE

Does the Bible say that he who repeats prayer shall receive much? No, he who *believes* shall be reckoned righteous, shall see prayer answered.

You recall Paul talking about his "thorn in the flesh," a harassment from Satan. He notes that it was so bad he prayed three times (2 Corinthians 12:8) for it to depart. Whoa! *Three times.* If a big problem provoked Paul to pray three times and note it in his epistle, this leads me to think that he usually entreated God one time about a need, perhaps twice for a serious problem. Jesus, too, at the Garden of Gethsemane, prayed three times, asking for the Father to remove what lay ahead. In each case, when they prayed three times, the answer was no.

Of course, we repeat because, like the slot machine player, we haven't hit the prize yet. No answer to prayer, at least none we can discern. God is not obliged to answer right away, or as soon as we hope. Maybe he wants to wait a while before giving his answer, but does he need a reminder in the meantime? I think not.

One of Scripture's greatest contrasts regarding this principle was Elijah's showdown with the prophets of Baal on Mount Carmel. Baal's prophets called upon him from morning until evening, with increasing frenzy. They hopped on the altar. They gashed themselves.

Then it was Elijah's turn. After stacking the odds further against God by having the sacrificial wood doused with water, he prayed one prayer. God answered. Fire came down from heaven.

The response of the Baal prophets was typical, in that most of the world's religions practice repetitive prayer. Considering that some of them are worshiping stone or wood images, it begins to make sense. Their deities are literally hard-headed. Our God is not. He is intelligent, and we are made in his image. We may fall short of hearing him, but he has no problem hearing us.

BUT WHAT ABOUT...?

If you are a good Bible student, you are raising some objections by this point.

Let's look at the persistent widow in Luke 18. The

judge said, "because this widow bothers me, I will give her legal protection, lest by continually coming she wear me out" (18:5). Jesus did not say we need to use her example as a way to pray, threatening to wear God out with our repetitions.

I believe we need to put the parable in context. Just prior to it, in Luke 17:20, Jesus begins a discussion about the coming of the kingdom of God in its fullness. As it moves into chapter 18, Luke explains the parable was "to show that at all times they ought to pray and not to lose heart" (18:1). After the parable, Jesus says, "However, when the Son of Man comes, will He find faith on the earth?" (18:8).

The widow was seeking protection from an adversary, and our adversary is the devil, as well as his manifestation on the earth. The church is like the widow, suffering injustice on an earth where Satan has broad reign; the church's continual prayer is "Lord, when will you bring relief from my adversary? When will you bring about justice?" It is not so much a prayer to be repeated as it is an attitude to be held steadfastly. There will not be justice on earth until the Lord returns. In the meanwhile, will we "lose heart"? No! "Faith on the earth" is what Jesus wants to see when he returns.

A similar parable is that of the persistent neighbor in Luke 11. This person goes to a neighbor at midnight seeking food for an unexpected guest. At first, the request is denied because it is so late. But then, "I tell you, even though he will not get up and give him anything because he is his friend, yet because of his persistence he will get up and give him as much as he needs" (11:8).

"Persistence" could also be translated here as "shamelessness" or "importunity." It was this person's shameless boldness, barging in at midnight, that is the key. As far as the length of the entreaty is concerned, it was probably just a matter of ten or fifteen minutes, not the months or years over which we may repeat a prayer. What I get from this parable is that Jesus wanted to emphasize that no time is the wrong time to pray, and that no request is too big.

Also, there is the matter of friendship. The neighbors' friendship was not enough to get that door open. Only boldness would do it. You must remember that you need not have completely right standing with God to approach him in prayer. Maybe you have strained your relationship with him by sin or inattentiveness. Don't lose hope. God's ear remains open to those shameless enough to call on him anyway.

Now you may see something different than I do in Jesus' parables, but I will finish with one explicit statement he made: "And when you are praying, do not use meaningless repetition, as the Gentiles do, for they suppose that they will be heard for their many words" (Matthew 6:7). This is the kind of God we serve, the God who voluntarily placed his life in us. He doesn't want our relationship reduced to "meaningless repetition," to boring lists, to predictable formulas. He wants ongoing dialog because he hears us the first time and has things he hopes we'll hear—if we're not too busy chattering.

10 || *Peace in Prayer*

THE WEDDING FEAST at Cana was as good as anyone could have hoped for. In fact, it was maybe too good—the festive guests had exhausted the wine supply.

Mary was there with Jesus. Even though his ministry had not blossomed, she knew that there might be something he could do about this little problem that no one else could.

"They have no wine," she told him. That's all. She didn't say, "Son, make wine."

We must understand the difference if we are to better understand prayer. *Mary stated the need; she did not dictate the solution.* She brought the problem to Jesus and trusted him with the outcome. Now the problem was out of her hands.

Mary's prayer demonstrates a key attitude in how we approach God: peace. The way of the flesh is to worry. It comes as natural as rebellion. We need no training to learn to worry. But we can all use some help in cultivating a heart of peace. As we do, that communication pathway between us and God will be so much smoother.

GOD'S PROVISION FOR PEACE

Isaiah 53:3 foreshadows Jesus: "He was despised and forsaken of men, a man of sorrows and acquainted with grief; and like one from whom men hide their face, he was despised, and we did not esteem Him." Why was this wonderful man Jesus despised and rejected? Why was he a man of sorrows, knowing grief so deeply? He never harmed anyone; in fact, he did just the opposite, healing so many. He did nothing to deserve the scorn and pain.

The following verses answer this dilemma: "Surely *our* griefs He Himself bore, and *our* sorrows He carried.... But He was pierced through for *our* transgressions, He was crushed for *our* iniquities; the chastening for *our* well-being fell upon Him, and by His scourging *we* are healed" (Isaiah 53:4-5).

So this intense suffering had nothing to do with Jesus, but with us. He didn't deserve it, but we do. He took the sorrows, the pain, the punishment we deserve because of sin and endured it all. He did it so that we might have well-being, or peace, or welfare.

Now that's all well and good, but you know that keeping your worry buttons turned off is not that simple. Satan will not leave alone what God has already accomplished.

He wants God's people to pay again for what God's Son already paid for. I still see so much worry among the people of God that I know there is a gap between the peace God has won for us and the peace the church has attained.

I am not saying Jesus died to deliver us from trouble. Nor am I saying that we should not feel pain. When a loved one dies, we should grieve. When we are sick, we're almost always going to hurt. We couldn't very well "weep with those who weep" (Romans 12:15) if there weren't something legitimate to cry about.

Job, for example, had a fat life. So Satan was quite sure that if God let him mess up Job's little paradise, Job would curse God. God accepted the bet, and we know how Job dug deep and found that there was something more lasting, more valuable than all the riches and cattle and children—a peace with God. It was a peace that accepted the bad with the good, knowing that God was in control.

Our experience with life is similar to Job's in that not all goes well. And this is true for everyone. But there should be something that sets us apart from those who don't know God. When everything goes wrong, we should have a different reaction, a different attitude. We have the peace of God. They don't.

NOT THE WORLD'S PEACE

Salvation is more than an insurance policy to keep us from having to accept uncomfortable surroundings in eternity. Salvation is for here and now. If we believe in the Son, we have eternal life—now—and we should start reflecting a bit of eternity in this temporal environment. Like Shadrach, Meshach and Abednego, we should be dancing amid the fire.

So what stops us? One problem is that we get confused about different kinds of peace. Jesus said, "Peace I leave with you; My peace I give to you; not as the world gives, do I give to you. Let not your heart be troubled, nor let it be fearful" (John 14:27).

The peace that the world gives is what you have if you have a good salary, no sickness, obedient children, a loving spouse, two new cars, a well-trained dog, and more cable TV stations than you can count. Even so, people with all these things, and much more, find that deep, lasting peace escapes them. But we know how the world *defines* peace in this way—an absence of surface trouble.

The peace Jesus gives "passes all comprehension" (Philippians 4:7). There is no outward reason to possess this peace. Every circumstance may be upside down, but you still have this elusive peace. It's what Paul and Silas had in jail. They had plenty of reason to complain. Or they could have been religious and prayed for God to release their feet from the stocks (you can bet they were pretty uncomfortable after an hour or two). Instead, they were praying and singing hymns to the same God whose business got them in this fix to begin with. Confronted with characters like this, it's little wonder that the jailer asked, "Sirs, what must I do to be saved?" (Acts 16:30). He knew they had something he didn't have.

Paul and Silas were able to give him that strange peace. Actually, though, mere men were not the source of this peace. As Jesus said, "*My* peace I give to you." The peace that Christ gives is founded in him and we cannot lose him once he comes to live in us. Yet how easy it is to lose the world's peace—children disappoint, marriages go sour, jobs suddenly end, sickness and death are inevitable, your faithful dog chews up the television cable right before your favorite show comes on. The very fragility of worldly peace makes it practically impossible to sit back and enjoy its fleeting appearances.

CASTING FOR PEACE

Though Jesus is the giver of peace, there is a role for us: to cast "all your anxiety upon Him, because He cares for you" (1 Peter 5:7). There comes a point where our will is involved. We choose to cast our worries on Jesus, or we choose to hoard them. Jesus is quite willing to take all our burdens; Scripture explains that his death took care of our sins as well as the worries that come in a fallen world.

Some people think this is complicated. They ask, "How *do* you do that?" Don't make it complex. When worries creep in, catch yourself and think, "Wait a minute —I'm worrying. I have every reason to worry, but I won't. I will cast all my anxieties on Jesus because he cares for me."

Most Christians think there are qualifications on what Peter said. Maybe, "Cast your cares upon him, but you better do something on your own because you know he really doesn't care a lick about you." Or, "Cast the big ones on him, but you better take care of the small ones." No, Peter said to cast *all* cares on Jesus. There is good reason for this, as we will see later, and it is not just to make us carefree.

Maybe you still don't see how you can actually cast those worries on God and make sure they don't bounce back on you, having grown larger during their brief absence. So let's look at the instruction booklet that comes with this special peace that passes understanding:

> Rejoice in the Lord always; again I will say, rejoice!... Be anxious for nothing, but in everything by prayer and supplication with thanksgiving let your requests be made known to God. And the peace of God, which surpasses all comprehension, shall guard your hearts and your minds in Christ Jesus. Finally, brethren, whatever is true, whatever is honorable, whatever is right, whatever is pure, whatever is lovely, whatever is of good repute, if there is any excellence and if anything worthy of praise, let your mind dwell on these things.
>
> **Philippians 4:4,6-8**

Rejoice! That's a good start. It may be hard to rejoice when you're worrying, but once you get in the rejoicing gear, worry doesn't seem to fit in.

Be anxious for nothing; in other words, *do not* be anxious. That's a commandment. If we let ourselves slide into worry and don't bother to climb out, it's sinful. Being anxious over big things is not something God winks at because "Be anxious for nothing" does not hedge on "nothing." But when the big worries come, or too many worries, there is more advanced instruction: "But in everything by prayer and supplication with thanksgiving let your requests be made known to God." When you take your problem in prayer to God, you don't have to take it back. That's why it says "with thanksgiving"—

when you know that it's in God's hands and you don't have to worry anymore, that's a lot to be grateful for.

When Satan starts looking for a crack in your mental and spiritual armor to slip that worry back in, imagine you are dealing with God as with a lawyer. Would you explain your case to a lawyer, pay a fee to hire him, then say, "Wait, let me take charge of this for a while. I'll think about it and worry some more to see if some miraculous solution will emerge"? I hope not.

Once we have deposited our worry at the foot of God's throne, we can expect the peace that surpasses understanding. We don't have to wait for circumstances to change, either. A spiritual and psychological peace is ours to enjoy not when we see the problem solved but as soon as we give the problem to God. Yet there is even more to be gained when we achieve victory over anxiety.

11 || *Dismantled by Worry*

I WAS SPEAKING AT A LEADERS' convention in the United States when someone interrupted me.

"Pastor Ortiz, how can you say, 'Don't worry' when the Ethiopians are dying of hunger?"

I said, "Are you worried about the Ethiopians?"

"Of course, I'm worried," he said.

"Well, quit worrying," I said. "Just write a large check and send it. And don't worry."

Doling out dollars is certainly not the answer to every need. Maybe God wants you to work in Ethiopia. Maybe he wants you to write letters to your congressman about sending aid. Maybe he doesn't want you even to think about the problems in Ethiopia. Just because you are aware of a big problem doesn't mean you have to play Messiah. The world's problems are bigger than your checkbook and longer than your day. Do what you believe you should do, and don't worry.

Now the man with the burden for Ethiopia felt he was doing something for them by worrying about it. This brings us to one of worry's tricks: You think you are actually doing something constructive by worrying. You're not. Don't kid yourself.

Remember, I promised to show you the bigger reason not to worry, the reason that transcends our own little furrowed brows. Here it is: *Worry takes us away from building the kingdom of God.*

OUT OF COMMISSION

But how easy it is to worry! When our son wanted to go to an expensive Christian college, my wife put on her worry robes.

"We can't afford it," she moaned. "What are we going to do?"

"Don't worry, sweetie, there is very little we can do," I said. "Let's make a list of what we can do. First, he can't go to that college."

"Oh, no!" she objected. "That's the one he really wants to attend."

"OK, let's sell our Steinway piano," I suggested.

"No, we can't do that. It is a gift from our parents," she said.

And so on. Nothing I suggested was workable, leaving only one apparent option—worry. But worry is not a solution, it is a dead-end.

So I decided to seek a loan from the bank.

"But how will we pay?" she asked.

"Shhh. Don't worry," I said.

We got the loan. We paid for it... and kept paying for it. But God enabled us to pay for it, and my son went to his college of choice. We did not starve or have to wear rags.

I told Martha, "You worried and I didn't, yet we ended up in the same place." Peace reigned in our house instead of worry.

Worrying is like this: You go to your garage, start your car, leave it in neutral and press the accelerator until the engine burns up. A lot of noise, a lot of energy expended, but you don't go anywhere. You end up worse off than before.

Worry puts us in neutral, too. We are useful for nothing while our mental and emotional engines are revving faster and faster. That's why worry is actually a kind of work, an internal labor. Even if you are lying in bed, worry will make you tired. Science has shown stress to be one of the major causes of disease, so there's a selfish payoff, too, in learning to fight stress by gaining peace of mind.

The worst part of being neutralized is that we become diverted from our commitment to build God's kingdom. Jesus understood this well, even in his day when there were no traffic jams and no one had ever heard of "stress management" courses. He said this:

"For this reason I say to you, do not be anxious for your life, as to what you shall eat, or what you shall drink; nor for your body, as to what you shall put on. Is not life more than food, and the body than clothing? Look at the birds of the air, that they do not sow, neither do they reap, nor gather into barns, and yet your heavenly Father feeds them. Are you not worth much more than they? And which of you by being anxious can add a single cubit to his life's span? And why are you anxious about clothing? Observe how the lilies of the field grow; they do not toil nor do they spin, yet I say to you that even Solomon in all his glory did not clothe himself like one of these. But if God so arrays the grass of the field, which is alive today and tomorrow is thrown into the furnace, will He not much more do so for you, O men of little faith? Do not be anxious then, saying, 'What shall we eat?' or 'What shall we drink?' or 'With what shall we clothe ourselves?' For all these things the Gentiles eagerly seek; for your heavenly Father knows that you need all these things. But seek first His kingdom and His righteousness; and all these things shall be added to you. Therefore do not be anxious for tomorrow; for tomorrow will care for itself. Each day has enough trouble of its own." **Matthew 6:25-34**

Now if you're tired of people like me saying, "Don't worry, don't worry," because you can't seem to grasp exactly what you *can* do in place of worrying, consider this passage. Jesus said to seek first God's kingdom, and all these other worry spots will fade away. He was saying, "I want to clean worry out of you so you can concentrate on the kingdom."

When personal matters consume you, do you care about working to establish God's kingdom? Do you care about the church? No, and that's the way Satan wants it. That's why worry is such a tremendous sin—it takes you off the front lines and puts you back in the hospital, waiting for a visit from the doctor. Not only are you out of commission, but you tend to suck other people's resources. "Brother, please pray for me... Pastor, I need this and that, what can you do...." You consume instead of produce.

I'm not saying you cannot bring your troubles, even the smallest of them, to God. He does care. He hears your prayers. But the more you have your worry under control, the more you can deal with the bumps and the mountains in your life. Some things, you learn to deposit with Jesus and forget about them before they become seeds of worry. You may find that other things need not be bothered with once your attention is focused on the higher purposes of God, his kingdom and his righteousness. Worry forces our attention away from the kingdom and onto our problems. Even if it's a big problem, it's small compared with the task of extending the kingdom.

SPOILING THE PARTY

> Now as they were traveling along, He entered a certain village; and a woman named Martha welcomed Him into her home. And she had a sister called Mary, who moreover was listening to the Lord's word, seated at His feet. But Martha was distracted with all her preparations; and she came up to Him, and said, "Lord do You not care that my sister has left me to do all the serving alone? Then tell her to help me." But the Lord answered and said to her, "Martha, Martha, you are worried and bothered about so many things; but only a few things are necessary, really only one, for Mary has chosen the good part, which shall not be taken away from her." **Luke 10:38-42**

Who invited Jesus in? Martha. So she was responsible for preparing the tea or whatever they had. The main problem was not that she was preparing things, but that she had a wrong attitude. She shook a big dose of worry salt over everything she was doing.

While Mary was sitting at Jesus' feet, I can imagine Martha talking to herself: "Just look at Mary, lounging around Jesus like she was a princess. She won't lift a hand to help. She won't even look this way. Who had to stoke the fire? Me. Who had to fill the teapot? Me. Who cut the bread? Me. And I suppose she expects me to carry all this in there, too. Well, I'm certainly not going to keep my mouth shut about this kind of treatment."

So Martha exploded. "Lord, do you not care that my sister has left me to do all the serving alone?"

Surprise, surprise: He didn't care. She was trying to drag Jesus into her problem, which was worry. After all, did Martha really need Mary in there with her? My wife always says that two people in the kitchen equals one too many.

Worry tends to spoil the party for everyone. Not only did Martha rebuke the wrong person, but she tried to manipulate Jesus into working out her grievance by commanding Mary to help. When we are worried, we feel that everybody should drop their business and pay attention to our concerns.

But Martha's entreaties did no good. I imagine their impromptu tea party unfolded with a lot of silence after Martha's outburst.

It didn't have to turn out this way. Martha could have thought, as she made preparations, "How nice that Mary is being blessed by my invitation of Jesus." Or if she were really that eager to hear what Jesus had to say, she could have invited them into the kitchen so they could all share the conversation while she fixed their snack.

But instead, Martha majored on worry. She may have been worried that she was getting the raw end of the deal—having to do too much by herself. Or that the preparations might not be as impressive as she wanted them to be. Or that Mary would gain too much fellowship or guidance or whatever Jesus had to offer, while she came in at the very end. But she was clearly worried, and her worry cast a pall over the gathering.

TEND THE SEED

When Jesus explained the parable of the sower, he said, "The seed which fell among thorns, these are the ones who have heard, and as they go on their way they are choked with worries and riches and pleasures of this life, and bring no fruit to maturity" (Luke 8:14).

This message about gaining peace is a seed. Worries will come to choke it out, and they will succeed unless you actively resist them, and seek first the kingdom of God. It's your choice. If you continue to choose to cast your anxieties upon Jesus, that seed will mature into a sturdy plant, much better able to resist the worries that would attempt to choke it.

12 || *Heaven's Junk Mail*

HAVE YOU EVER FOUND YOURSELF bartering with God? You pray fifteen minutes a day, for example, and you assume (though you don't admit this to God) that he will bless you. Step it up to a half hour and add a Bible chapter every day, and you can expect, oh, a good pay raise on top of your other blessings. Throw in some fasting here and there, and hoo boy! No telling what sort of payoff is in the works.

Now why do we think prayer is a coin with which we can buy things from God? Is it because we think it is a sacrifice, something that costs us, a little part-time chore that's so unpleasant that we naturally expect something in return? Well, if you see prayer that way, I can't blame you for having such expectations. But as we are seeing, this is not God's idea of prayer.

This matter of having improper motives in how we

approach God underlies one more problem with prayer—
our belief that God is our servant.

GIVING ORDERS

Every parent knows that one big difference between
children and adults is that children are continually asking,
adults are continually giving. Consequently, one key step
to maturity is moving from an asking mentality to a giving
mentality.

Examine your prayer life. When you are subcon-
sciously expecting God to bless you in proportion to the
amount of time you spend in prayer, or when you expect
him to answer your prayer because you've repeated it so
often, your prayer life probably consists primarily of
works and merits. After all, why give up time in your busy
day to send paperless telegrams up to the sky unless you
are going to get something worthwhile? Health, wealth,
family peace—you know the basics on everyone's list.

I'm not telling you to refrain from asking God for
things. But bear with me and you will see there is much
more to the mature Christian prayer life.

The Bible talks a lot about servants and masters. In our
relationship with God, who is the servant and who is the
master? We say we are the servants, but do we act like it?
Who gives the orders to whom? See if this sounds similar
to your own prayers or those in your Sunday school class
or home fellowship group:

"Dear Father, while I'm away from home, take care of
my house so no thieves come in."

"Yes, madam," we imagine him saying.

"Lord, watch over me as I drive out of town so that I don't have any accidents."

"Yes, sir."

"Father, my mother is in the hospital. Please help the doctors when they conduct the operation."

"Absolutely."

"Lord, my son is in college. Help him with his grades."

"No problem."

"Lord, my husband must find a better job because you know how we need more money."

"I'll see what I can do about it."

"Jesus, you know how I hate to walk and how late I am arriving for church. Please make sure there is a parking place close to the door."

"But of course."

It sounds as if "*My* will be done in heaven as it is on earth," is what Jesus taught us to pray. But he didn't. He said to pray, "*Thy* will be done on earth as it is in heaven."

Again, there is a balance here. We should bring requests to God. There is no law that says a master cannot do something kind for a servant. But our natural tendency is to shift the balance way over to our side, to make God a Santa Claus who will magically answer every wish on our list. Especially if we have been acting like good children.

TRUE SERVANTS

When you think of "servant," do you picture a sedate philosopher or a farm hand? A cook or someone busy at work? That you are put in the place of servant should automatically impact your prayer life. If you are praying, praying, praying, and keep waiting, waiting, waiting for

God to do something, check yourself. The words may be rushing out of your mouth like water down a mountain stream, but something may be clogging your spiritual ears.

"Lord, brother Joseph lost his job. Oh, dear Lord, he lost his job!"

"Gosh, thanks for the news!" Is that how God responds? No. He knew about brother Joseph's job situation before brother Joseph got the word. God is interested in prayer more like this:

"Lord, as you know, brother Joseph lost his job. What would you like me to do? I'm your servant."

"Go to the store and buy one bag of groceries and take it to his house in my name."

So you do it. "Brother Joseph, in the name of Jesus, such as I have, I give you."

After I preached this in Los Angeles, a woman gave a testimony the next day.

"This morning as I went over my prayer list, I said, 'Lord, you are the Lord and I am your servant. My first request is for my friend that moved to New York. I've been praying for her every day. What would you like me to do?'

"'Call her,' said the Lord.

"'Hello, this is your friend from California.... No, nobody died. I'm calling because I was remembering you and I love you. No, I have no news. I just wanted to see how you are. I'm calling because I like you.'"

This woman said her friend explained how she had been depressed for two weeks and was contemplating suicide. Just knowing that a friend cared enough to call, and sharing their prayer together on the phone, made a tremendous difference for her. Present yourself to God as his servant, and you can bet he will find a thing or two for you to do.

SPIRITUAL HUNGER STRIKES

I used to find myself bargaining with God, even demanding things, especially in fasting. I felt like I was pulling out all the stops; God could not help but answer. "Lord, here's your promise," I would say. "You have said it. You ought to do it."

Finally, he could reply, "Juan Carlos, let me remind you of my requests to you, and the fact that you haven't done any of them."

Many times I fasted two weeks; sometimes I ended up in the hospital. Too often I approached fasting as another bargaining tool. I wanted something. That is not a fast— it's a hunger strike. It's like trying to twist someone's arm to do exactly what you want.

Now I have learned what God intended fasting to be. In combination with normal prayer, it is *a weakening of our flesh so our spirit can discern better God's will for us.* Its purpose is to sharpen the ear of the servant so the Master's voice comes in crystal clear.

Have you ever had a bad case of flu or something else that put you in bed for days at a time? And it turned out to be a spiritual blessing because you had a lot of time to think, to pray, to come to understand things that you had been missing? Sometimes God has to allow us to get sick in bed with an illness because it's the only way to get us to look upward without falling asleep.

That's the way fasting is. It's a kind of sickening yourself artificially by becoming so weak you cannot run, you cannot push yourself too much. You have to be quiet and keep your movements to a minimum or else you will get dizzy. Fasting won't usually result in major revelations, but it can make you more meditative so that you begin to better understand yourself and the situations God has placed you in. You can sense God's will more accurately.

Of course, there are exceptions. Esther correctly sensed a burden from God about a threat that could have wiped his chosen people off the earth, and she proclaimed a fast. She was fasting to get something—deliverance—and was right on target. You may find yourself with a similar burden, though it will be less important than Esther's, and the Holy Spirit makes known to you that a fast would be in order. Obey. But do not make fasting into the atomic bomb of spiritual warfare—the last, biggest, most effective weapon that we must unveil when we want something to happen. Fasting is a hearing aid more than it is a weapon.

WHO'S YOUR LOVER?

The root problem here is one of motives. Consider the admonition of James 4:3-5:

> You ask and do not receive, because you ask with wrong motives, so that you may spend it on your pleasures. You adulteresses, do you not know that friendship with the world is hostility toward God? Therefore whoever wishes to be a friend of the world makes him-

self an enemy of God. Or do you think that the Scripture speaks to no purpose: "He jealously desires the Spirit which He has made to dwell in us"?

God placed his Spirit in us, yet he's jealous—jealous of the world. God came to dwell within us so from within us he could use our bodies for his kingdom purposes. So our feet would be the beautiful feet on the mountain that brings good news. So our minds would become the mind of Christ.

But there is much for him to be jealous about. We flirt so much with the world. I'm not talking about the obvious big sins—adultery and so on. I'm talking about the baubles of the world, our busy-ness with the world.

"Lord, I need a new car. Help me buy that car."

"Oh, God, you know how I need a VCR. Even the pastor has a VCR, so it can't be all bad. And you know I'll watch Christian teaching tapes."

Our mouths say "Lord" but our hearts are beating to the rhythm of the world. God hears the distinction quite clearly, and he's jealous. We get consumed with passion for our other lover, and our time, our money, just doesn't seem to stretch far enough for the Lord. Yet we're so eager for God to stretch a little further for us. Meanwhile, the Lord keeps waiting for us to return. Sometimes our prayers are like a woman asking her husband, "Darling, please give me some money so I can spend the weekend at a nice hotel with my secret lover."

This is what James is talking about: You ask with the wrong motives, especially the motive of spending it on your pleasures. Therefore, you are an adulteress—you turn from your first true love.

That's why so many of our prayers are what I call the junk mail of heaven. It's not illegal or anything. God could answer it if he wanted to, but he knows—so much better than we do—that his purposes will not be best served by answering the deluge of junk mail that comes his way.

How different it is to pray, "Lord, why don't you give someone in our church the gift of giving so your resources can be unleashed here and this need can be met. Please release the gift of healing here so that others can see your power and come to repentance."

The truest satisfaction of a servant is to see his master satisfied. We can make self-centered requests for things of the world all day long, and God may even answer some of our requests. But this is not asking with the right motivation, and we cannot expect this sort of prayer exercise to lead us to much maturity.

Jesus said to be faithful in the small things. This includes prayer. Approach God as a servant, listen to *his* needs, and be faithful in the mundane: Take groceries to the family without a job; bathe the children of sister Mary who is sick in bed; give twenty dollars to your neighbor who has a run of misfortune.

Instead of presenting your conventional prayer list reflecting all your needs, list what you believe God wants to use you for. Let Jesus use your hands, your legs, your mind, your compassion, your wallet, your time. You'll be amazed at how much God answers prayers when you come to him with the right motives, and how this frees you up for what we'll see are his higher purposes.

13 || *Beyond Petitions*

Aɴʏ ᴘᴀʀᴇɴᴛ ᴏꜰ ᴍᴏʀᴇ than one child knows that where two or more are gathered, you can expect an argument. I remember the special occasions where we would serve Coca-Cola at our dinner table in Argentina. Little eyes would watch how much was poured into each glass.

"Daddy, she got more than I did!" one would say.

"Yes, but I'm older," she would respond.

Then a third, "But last time you got more than I did."

I did not harshly judge in those circumstances. But if my wife and I were to argue over an inch of soft drink, it would be another story.

The difference is one of maturity. As I mentioned, in the growing-up process we gradually move from asking to giving. When we apply this to spiritual matters, we must then consider a person's spiritual age. That's why it's not

necessarily wrong for God's people to ask him for things
of the world, things for themselves. One Christian may be
in more of a baby-to-Daddy relationship than another,
even though salvation occurred many years ago. But the
normal path is for each of us to move toward maturity.

What happens as we mature in Christ is that we can
combine some of the elements of the Christian walk that
we have examined—forgiveness, peace, flowing fellowship with God, a servant's attitude and self-control—to
produce a better, more common-sensical prayer life. This
becomes much more effective than mindless repetitions
of prayer lists or frequent hunger strikes. We'll see that
not only our prayer, but the actions prayer motivates us to
undertake, will open up an entirely new world.

COMMON SENSE

Once a woman asked my advice about a confusing
mess in which God was not answering prayer.

"Brother Ortiz, my husband has run away with a
woman from the church. And I have two children," she
said. The ex-husband's mother also was involved, and
there appeared to be no easy answer except for this
woman to shoot the happy new couple.

Well, the church had put together a prayer group of
about a dozen people who had all come with this woman
to see me. They had been praying for weeks, and their
big question was: How long should they continue?

God gave us no time limits on prayer, but he gave us
one wonderful gift—the mind. We often have to engage
our common sense in concert with our prayer life to make

sure we don't get led down some spiritual dead-end.

So I told these women, "Make a list of all the people involved—you, your ex-husband, your children, his mother, the other woman," and so on. "Then ask the Lord, 'What shall I do about my husband? Will he come back to me or not? Should I keep waiting?'"

After all, God is your friend. Why would he want to hide important things from you?

"If God says no about your husband's return, then cross your husband off your list and forget about him. Look for another man or decide to stay single, but be sure to forget about him.

"Ask God about your children. 'What should I tell them, Lord?'

"What about the other woman? 'Lord, can I go tell her what I think of her?' Probably you can. Then forget about her." That is the point where peace should replace your worries.

If these women looked no further than at their desired answer for their friend's problem, it would be as if they expected God to do all the things that the woman needed to do, but that she was putting off. We can become so focused on our own expectations that we miss God's provision.

Imagine a man who climbs on top of his roof to escape a flood. Another man arrives in a boat and says, "Come on! We'll take you to safety."

The roof-sitter says, "No, I'm trusting the Lord for deliverance." And the water rises a little more.

Then a helicopter comes and drops a lifeline. He hollers back, "No thanks, I'm trusting the Lord for help."

An hour later he is floating among the logs and he is

complaining to God in heaven.

"I trusted you, God. Why didn't you save me?"

"I'm a little confused," God replies. "I sent you a boat and a helicopter, but you refused my help."

God gave us a brain partly so that he could fellowship with us. This means he expects prayer to be a fluid, surprising thing. Unless we are using that computer on top of our shoulders, we will struggle with our prayers and their apparent futility.

SENSE ENOUGH TO ACT

We need to use common sense when it comes to figuring out what we can do something about and what we can't.

Suppose you pray for the salvation of someone you know. God probably will not work some hocus-pocus, overnight change of heart in that person. He usually works by sending at least one person who manifests the love of Christ in a way that opens the door for salvation. If you have enough of a burden to pray for the person, you may well be the one to befriend her. And that doesn't mean talking about the weather for a few minutes and then dropping the four spiritual laws on her. Get to know her by sharing a meal, playing a sport together, going somewhere you both enjoy.

Remember, you are the servant, not God. When the Master wants you about his work, don't hide behind prayer. If your task meets what seems like failure, don't despair if you are being faithful to do God's bidding.

At other times, you may have a burden for someone's salvation, and you need to check your common sense to discover that there is nothing much you can do about it. One of my children, upon reaching young adulthood, was only a superficial Christian. It concerned Martha and me. We prayed in the child's bedroom to rebuke any evil influences, which was a good step to take. But beyond that, we sensed that God mainly wanted us to extend our love.

So one day I said, "Listen, I will never rebuke you again because then our relationship would deteriorate and we would always be fighting, and you already know what I think is right and wrong. We'll just be kind to you and kiss you and hug you. We'll do that because we love you, but not because we agree with you."

And then my wife was able to let this rest in the Lord's hands. She shed no more tears over it. We gained peace, and the child's spiritual walk began to improve, until he became a committed Christian.

IS THIS REALLY PRAYER?

We are talking about moving into greater maturity in prayer, so let's look at some prayer examples in the New Testament. You will be surprised—some of these do not look like prayers. Maybe they are not prayers, in a sense. But they achieved the kind of results that would cause most of us to jump up and down, even if we got results in only five percent of our prayer requests.

"But Peter said, 'I do not possess silver and gold, but what I do have I give to you: In the name of Jesus Christ the Nazarene—walk!' And seizing him by the right hand, he raised him up; and immediately his feet and his ankles were strengthened" (Acts 3:6-7).

Was Peter praying? Did he say, "Heavenly Father, we

come into your presence to ask healing for this poor sick person. Stretch forth your hand!" If what we practice as prayer is truly prayer, then Peter was not praying, he was grandstanding. After all, he mentioned Jesus, but did not ask Jesus or the Father to do anything. Maybe Peter's was a prayer of faith, and our typical prayer is one of doubt.

Peter remembered what we seem to forget: that God dwells within us. That's why he could confidently proclaim "what I do have I give to you." You bet he had something. And he was willing to use it.

Peter acted with similar authority later on. In Acts 5, everyone in the church was selling their possessions and bringing the whole amount to the apostles' feet, as unto Christ. Ananias sold his house, but it appears he did so under the pressure of conforming to what everyone else was doing. He shows up with proceeds from the sale of his house, acting like it's the whole bundle.

I imagine that Peter at first saw the big offering and said, "Halleluia! Praise the Lord for this nice sum."

Then the Lord spoke to Peter, "Don't be glad. That man is a deceiver."

"What do you mean, Lord?"

"He will tell you he sold the house for 50,000 shekels, but he sold it for 100,000. As soon as he tells the lie, I want him to drop dead."

"Oh, Lord, you must want to teach a lesson for the whole church."

And so it happened. He lied, he died—right on the spot. No need for the Sunday night Bible lesson.

When Ananias' wife, Sapphira, showed up, Peter confronted her with their scheme. Peter said, "Behold, the feet of those who have buried your husband are at the door, and they shall carry you out as well" (Acts 5:9). And she died just as Peter predicted.

Peter did not pray, "Lord, kill her!" Nor did he get religious, saying, "In the holy name of Jesus, Lord render asunder today this woman's body and spirit."

Basically, he pronounced a death sentence. He didn't even include "in the name of Jesus." Was it prayer? I don't care what you call it, but it showed a man open to hearing from God, and then speaking and acting upon what he heard. There would be no stopping the growth of God's kingdom if all his people were tuned in and obedient like Peter was in that circumstance.

Peter acted boldly again in Acts 9. Aeneas had been paralyzed and bedridden eight years. "Peter said to him, 'Aeneas, Jesus Christ heals you; arise, and make your bed.' And immediately he arose" (Acts 9:34). What's often not recorded in scripture is the inner dialogue I believe usually occurred before such miracles. The Holy Spirit probably told Peter to heal Aeneas.

Acting upon that kind of conversation, Peter and his cohorts had a good success rate. They were declaring prayers of faith. "Now faith is the assurance of things hoped for, the conviction of things not seen" (Hebrews 11:1). So a prayer of faith is something we are fairly sure of. That assurance, that conviction, has to come from the Spirit.

RAISING THE DEAD

Move up to the end of Acts 9 and Peter is in the big leagues when it comes to miracles—he's faced with raising the dead. Tabitha, also known as Dorcas, a very godly woman, had died. The Bible doesn't provide much detail about the actual healing. Maybe the mourners simply asked Peter to raise her from the dead, and he did. I think Peter experienced something more like this:

"Peter, raise her up," said the Lord.

"But Lord, she's dead! Really dead!"

"I want you to raise her up and display my power."

"But I touched her, and she's cold," objected Peter. "I mean, she's not just passed out or almost dead, she's really gone. You're talking about a lot more than just healing people."

"That's OK," said the Lord. "I'll do my part. You do yours."

"Well, all right." So Peter—and this is not my imagination—"sent them all out" of the room (Acts 9:40). I can't blame him for not wanting an audience. So then it was just Peter, the Lord, and a stiff, cold corpse.

"Lord, come on. Now that I've sent these people out, they're going to be expecting something eye-popping when I open the door. Don't make me a laughingstock."

"Yes, Peter, I told you to raise her and I meant it."

Finally he said, "Tabitha, arise," (9:40) and she did.

What's not exactly spelled out in the Bible is that Peter, Paul, and the other disciples were not healing every single sick person everywhere they went. Even Jesus didn't, and he knew he wasn't supposed to. Remember that he said that he couldn't work many miracles because of the people's lack of faith. That's because he was in complete submission to the Father, and the Father's intent was not to spread a blanket of miracles over the whole earth.

DON'T TRY TO GIVE WHAT YOU DON'T HAVE

Raising someone from the dead is a spectacular thing, and is not recorded too many times in the Bible. Nevertheless, it is there, and Jesus promised we would do greater things than he did. So why do we not see this phenomenon happen more often?

Once I was at a funeral for a young boy who had died in an accident, so it was particularly sad. The parents were getting extremely emotional. I was a young pastor, and wasn't sure exactly what I could, or should do. So, when nobody was watching, I went to the corpse and said, "In the name of Jesus, get up!" Nothing. I said, "Lord, why this? Why can't he live? It doesn't seem just. What can I tell the parents?"

I let the matter drop. About a half hour later, still in the funeral, the Lord seemed to ask me, "Juan Carlos, do you want to know why you didn't raise that boy?"

"Why?"

"Because I haven't given you that gift. But I know you have $100 in your pocket that could help this family tremendously with the funeral expenses. Give what you have and don't try to give what you don't have."

So I went to the father and said, "Brother, such as I have I give you. In the name of Jesus, have this $100." It was a help.

Remember Peter's words to the lame man—"What I do have I give to you." All Christians have Jesus, but beyond that we do not all have the same material or spiritual gifts. God equips us differently. This applies not just to raising the dead, but to any situation.

So I encourage you, ask of God what you need to ask,

but do not limit prayer to asking, especially asking only for personal needs. We have a communicative God, who desires continual fellowship with us—praising, worshiping, thanksgiving—and all of these things spring from the give and take of prayer. We will mature in our prayer life only as we cultivate our relationship with the God who dwells within us. Let's learn more about what it means to have that new life within.

14 | *Life or Laws?*

SUPPOSE I AM praying today and the Holy Spirit tells me to eat an orange. Halleluia! The Spirit has led me! So I consume an orange. In my prayer notebook I write, "God desires me to eat oranges. I must always have oranges on hand to fulfill my duty to God." In my spirit, I sense the fulfillment of having heard from God and obeyed him. All is well.

The next day, my spirit is less eager to tune in to God's Spirit. Why should I care? I already have a constitution for my new denomination, The Orange Church.

But the Lord is persistent. "Juan Carlos, eat an apple."

An apple? That voice must be Satan's. I know that God's clear revelation, tested by experience, is that oranges are sacred food. And so begins the separation of my well-intentioned Christian walk from the intentions of God.

Does this story, strange as it is, sound familiar? It should. This tendency to institutionalize the new, the spontaneous, the fresh, is part of human nature. It happens not just in churches, but throughout society. You can see it in clubs and associations and movements everywhere.

And institutionalization is not all bad. What should concern us, though, is that God wants us interested in things not of human nature, but of Spirit nature. We have seen how God dwells with us, a Spirit mingling with our spirits, and this should affect how we pray and act. That new life is there always, not just in worship or fellowship or prayer, but always. What I want to address for a few chapters is the growth of that life—or more commonly, the things that keep it from growing. God's seed in us should be constantly maturing, changing the church as it changes us.

READY OR NOT?

I have written before about the problem of spiritual immaturity. How much the church has suffered because babes in Christ have not been called to grow up, have not been challenged to move on to adulthood in Christ. I want to revisit this area in the light of the understanding that God is closer than we think. Indeed, his life is in us; but is that *life* what makes us tick, or are we driven by something else?

Let's review 1 Corinthians 3:1-3:

And I, brethren, could not speak to you as to spiritual men, but as to men of flesh, as to babes in Christ. I gave you milk to drink, not solid food; for you were not yet able to receive it. Indeed, even now you are not yet able, for you are still fleshly. For since there is jealousy and strife among you, are you not fleshly, and are you not walking like mere men?

What a pity! Paul could not address the church as spiritual creatures because they were basically on the fleshly level. They had not matured. They would have to miss deeper truth simply because they couldn't handle it.

Could the same thing happen in today's churches? That our pastor has many degrees and speaks eloquently does not mean that we are getting spiritual meat instead of milk. That we are college graduates and can follow all that he says does not mean we are munching on spiritual steak. That we have been in a church twenty years does not guarantee spiritual adulthood.

God, in his love, acts like Paul did. He simply does not reveal more than we can stand. A small table can support a glass of water or a vase of flowers, but a Cadillac placed on top of it would turn it into splinters.

Think of the more outward spiritual gifts. God can distribute them wherever he chooses, but he is wise to be selective. A gun can be used beneficially for hunting, but a wise parent does not let children play with a real gun. Imagine if many people in the church today had the gift, as Paul demonstrated with Elymas the sorcerer, of making people blind. Each denomination would be zapping the other in the name of Jesus. Soon the whole church would be stumbling around while the rest of the world whistled along.

This is one reason God is slow to reveal more about

himself. Every time he does, there is a risk—perhaps I should say a likelihood—of division. Study church history and you'll see that every time there was new light, there was a problem. The basic cause of division was immaturity on behalf of a big part of the church.

RESISTING CHANGE

What exactly is immaturity? It is someone or something that hasn't changed with time. Immaturity reflects a resistance to change. When Scripture speaks of a hard heart, it's talking about a person set in stone, opposed to internal change.

After I had been in the United States and seen the collection plates that were used in church, I proposed the idea to my congregation in Argentina. We had been using long bags strung poorly with wire on old broom handles. Our deacons looked like they were hunting butterflies when they walked around with those sacks. Our church had become a little more sophisticated, and I thought the change would be appropriate.

But no! "Pastor, you know the founder of the church made those bags," the deacons said. We argued and argued. But we couldn't change things.

It was as if there were a Law of Collection Equipment, an obscure verse in Deuteronomy promising that fire would pour out of heaven on those who dared to substitute anything for the tithe receptacle. This touches the heart of the problem: Is the church only an *institution* ruled by laws, constitutions, and decrees? Or is it also an *organism* ruled by life? Let's examine the differences between the two.

When an institution is formed, some kind of charter or constitution gets drafted. It spells out what the group believes and does, how it will be ruled, and so on. Nothing is left to chance. If something gets left out, an amendment gets passed. I am not saying this is bad. It works fine for governments and many other institutions. To a degree, it even works for churches, but it also brings built-in problems.

In our denominations, chances are we won't be exposed to certain teachings because they don't fit our group's mold. Everything has been thought out. Everything concerning God's truth has been established. Even if you, a loyal member, believe you have received some light or something fresh that would benefit your brothers and sisters, you may not be allowed to discuss what God has shown you. We may profess to remain flexible to God, but underneath the skin a hardening of the arteries has set in.

Two very similar things have happened in such cases. Both involve the ears—the ears of the heart, that is. One is that we members of an institution tend to become *dull of hearing*, which will be examined in the next chapter. The other is that we become *lazy of hearing*. When we believe we have all the basic truth, why should we listen to anything else? A good sermon for us is simply the most entertaining, non-challenging way to present old truth.

I'm not telling you to leave your denomination; I belong to one myself. But there are certain pitfalls to be aware of. Our denominations tend to look over their shoulders and shake their heads. Pentecostals look at Presbyterians and think, "They are not Spirit-filled." Presbyterians think of the Pentecostals, "Poor people; they have a shallow theology." And on and on. This kind of attitude is a great hindrance for growth. People with such a mindset become unteachable.

Consider 1 Corinthians 8:1-2: "Knowledge makes arrogant, but love edifies. If anyone supposes that he knows anything, he has not yet known as he ought to know." This humility is critical for growth. Furthermore, without it we tend to offend our brothers and sisters in Christ. Think of the term "full gospel." If we put that in a church or ministry name, does it mean we think we have the whole truth but everyone else has some fraction? I hope not. But it sure sounds like it.

I was invited to a United Methodist convention in California. They made a point of letting me know they were liberals, and tried to help me correct my language. They told me not to say mankind, but humankind. Don't refer to God as Father or he, but as Mother or Father, or he and she.

Now you could say that I am liberal in the sense that I am open to God's change, but this sort of talk strained even my sensibilities. Yet I tell you, these were beautiful people. I learned a lot from them.

Six or seven of us in a prayer group were given the topic of suffering to discuss from the book of Job. Everyone spoke about all the suffering in the world, so when my turn came, I shifted the emphasis.

"Listen, I believe that most of the suffering is brought by Satan," I said.

One pastor said, "You mean by a negative force." I remembered that I was mixing with liberals, and this one apparently did not believe in Satan.

Then another pastor came to my rescue and addressed the skeptic. "Brother, I always believed like you—that there is no Satan—but two years ago a lady from my church came running to my office, saying, 'Please, Pastor, come! My daughter is under demonic possession. Come and pray for her.' So I went to my office. I took an old Episcopalian book on exorcism and I went and I exorcised the girl and she got delivered. Since that day I believe there is a Satan and I cast out demons."

You know what the doubting man answered? "Well, a theory is good until proven the opposite. I believe I have to revise my theory about Satan." He was so open. He was not too lazy to hear something fresh from God through other people. I said to myself, "My goodness! These liberals are a good group to come to, to sow seeds with, and to learn."

Do you know what happens if you go to a more fundamentalist meeting and you share something at odds with what people believe? You will probably get thrown out. Expect no revision of theory. Liberals such as those I met with are in one sense more open than conservative Christians who are so certain they have all the right doctrine. This is the danger of the church functioning only as an institution: *Unconsciously, we do not see what our church system doesn't want us to see.*

This is enough of a problem by itself. But read on, and you will see that there is even more at work to undermine our audio-spiritual system. As long as Satan can succeed there, he doesn't have to worry that the new life of Christ in each of us will ever grow past the nursery stage.

15 | *Have We Become Hard of Hearing?*

Closely related to the problem of being too lazy to hear is the tendency of people who are comfortable in an institution to become *dull of hearing*. What dulls the hearing? Traditionalism.

It didn't take long for this problem to make itself known in the church. It's a good thing it arose early because the stakes were high.

Peter and the other disciples were Jews from head to toe. Circumcised, well-versed in the Law, they knew they were the best, the elect, God's chosen people for eternity.

What they didn't know is that they were wrong.

For all their knowledge, all the intimacy of having walked the earth with Jesus, they did not fully comprehend what he had accomplished.

We know that about a number of things Jesus was pretty clear. "Go therefore and make disciples of all the nations," he said in Matthew 28:19. "You shall be my witnesses... even to the remotest part of the earth" (Acts 1:8). And I bet Jesus said many other things to make his intentions clear about the universality of the gospel.

When he was gone, did the disciples have the idea of preaching to the Gentiles? No. Yet Peter, James, John, and the rest had been in the front row when Jesus was giving instructions. They were probably the loudest with "Amen! Preach it! Halleluia! We receive it, Lord!"

When Jesus told the parables about being dull of hearing, they probably heard them the same way Christians today tend to hear them—"Yes, others really are hard of hearing when it comes to spiritual matters. Thank God we have been enlightened."

Off they went after Jesus' ascension, preaching to fellow chosen people, healing and seeing good success. But their mission was less than what God wanted. He got tired of their dullness, a dullness that resulted from centuries of Jewish tradition and pride.

HELP FROM ON HIGH

So God sent an angel to Cornelius, a Gentile. The angel instructed him to send soldiers and to retrieve Peter. Peter, meanwhile, was having a strange dream from the Lord. A blanket suddenly appeared on which were reptiles and birds and other animals Jews were forbidden to eat. A voice told Peter to kill them and eat. The voice of tradition so deeply rooted in Peter resisted, saying, in effect, "No, Lord! You know we don't do things that way in our denomination." Three times God showed Peter the blanket of creatures, but Peter's tradition had him bound too strongly to be open to something new.

God then warned Peter that Cornelius' men would be coming and—I think God was simply taking no chances with Peter's unbounded stubbornness—told him to go with them. The men came and informed Peter that Cornelius was led by an angel to seek a message from Peter.

Peter must have known God was at work here. First, he had this vision three times in a row. Then the messengers spoke of an angelic appearance that coincided with Peter's vision. Peter, showing up at Cornelius' place, even went as far as acknowledging that "God has shown me that I should not call any man unholy or unclean," (Acts 10:28) though he was merely explaining that he, a holy Jew, was willing to commit the no-no of setting foot inside a Gentile's house.

What Peter said next was astounding, coming from the man who was so quick to speak rashly for Jesus, to walk on the water when no one else would: "And so I ask for what reason you have sent for me" (Acts 10:29).

If you had a vision from God that seemed to imply a breaking down of barriers, then a neighbor you didn't know very well showed up at your door saying an angel informed him that you had a divine word for him, would you think that maybe, just maybe, this was an opportunity to witness?

Peter could not yet arrive at that conclusion. It took this crazy sequence of events before the light bulb flashed on in his head. He finally admitted that "God is not one to show partiality, but in every nation the man who fears Him and does what is right, is welcome to Him" (Acts 10:34-35).

Even at this point, I believe he was not planning to offer baptism to these Gentiles. I imagine the Father and Son in heaven, saying, "Look at old Peter. He's probably going to blow it again—lay this big gospel message on them and then walk out, leaving everybody condemned. We better make things even more obvious."

While Peter was still speaking, the Holy Spirit fell. All the Jewish believers were amazed because these Gentiles were speaking in tongues, praising God, and having a rip-roaring Holy Ghost meeting (Acts 10:44-46).

I bet Peter grabbed his cohorts and went into another room for an impromptu board meeting.

"What are we going to do?" said Peter.

"Should we baptize them, or what?" said another.

"We could, but what would the brethren in Jerusalem say?" said a third.

By then God's angels blared in Peter's ear: "Baptize them! Baptize them!"

"I sense God would have us baptize them," Peter announced. So they did.

CLINGING TO TRADITION

God finally got his message across in spite of dear Peter. We must not judge him too harshly; it was beyond him, without God's help, to shake the traditions of centuries. And it wasn't just Peter. When he got back to Jerusalem, he had to convince the elders there of the same thing, which took some fancy talking.

Tradition isn't always wrong. But traditionalism is so powerful, sometimes dulling our ability to hear God and his written word. Preying upon our fleshly desire for familiarity, for comfort, for eliminating embarrassing surprises, traditionalism can be a prime tool of Satan. Many Christians would rather give up the Bible than their human traditions.

This is why Jesus had no kind words for mere human tradition. When the Pharisees started needling him about his disciples' failure to wash their hands when they ate bread, you could almost feel his blood pressure rising: "And why do you yourselves transgress the commandment of God for the sake of your tradition?" (Matthew 15:3). Then he gives the example of their dodging their parents' financial needs by giving money for religious use, and thereby violating the commandment to honor their parents.

THE MOLDABLE CHURCH

Human traditions thrive in an institution because an institution usually doesn't really change. It may get a new building or new leaders, it may be bigger or smaller, but it stays the same.

An organism is more complex. It changes substantially, yet, in a certain respect, it doesn't change at all. This is why the church should be more like an organism. The church is made up of people, people who have died to their flesh-and-blood lives and are being transformed into the life of Christ. In one sense, the church should not change because Jesus Christ is the same yesterday, today, and forever. The Father, Son, and Spirit are eternal. Their nature is eternal. Their principles are eternal. God's revealed word has eternal application.

On the other hand, the church—like a true organism—should change. Consider how a family grows and matures. At first, my children were concerned only with childish things. Now they are grown and handling adult responsibilities, caring for their own homes and families, earning a living, and so on.

Each child is still a human being. Each one is still an Ortiz offspring. Each one retains personality traits, convictions, and hints of facial characteristics they had growing up. Yet they are remarkably different from the squealing, crawling, toddlers I once knew. They have changed. Fortunately, no human tradition is strong enough to block change in what is truly an organism.

WHAT RULES?

Another difference between institutions and organisms is what rules them.

An inner life rules an organism. Organisms, when they are young, get bigger as part of the growth process. There is a continual pushing, an expansion. A genetic code determines the changes an organism will go through, and only death or severe disease will stand in the way.

Laws rule an institution. In many church institutions, if you believe in the resurrection, the second coming, and whatever other doctrines are stressed, and you don't smoke, don't drink, and don't go to the movies or whatever else is on the naughty list, you are OK. Pay tithes and come to meetings and work in the church, and you are more than OK. With members like this, institutions just float along, oblivious to pushing, unless the pushing comes from within and then it becomes too much to bear.

God still pushes today. Even in Pentecostal and other churches, where leaders emphasize being open to moves of the Spirit, enough rigidity creeps in for resistance to become a problem. Unfortunately, the side effect of a successful shove from God is that some people get knocked down and left dazed and confused, sometimes becoming bitter in the process.

I don't mean to be negative about denominationalism, but because we are all driven by a desire to find a place where we can hang our mind up on the rack and put our body, soul and spirit on cruise control, denominations run the risk of stagnating.

Lest you think this is simply my raving, look at Jesus. With whom did he spend most of his time? Sinners, prostitutes, publicans—those outside the law. They had no pretenses of righteousness. They did not have Truth all figured out.

He never told Gentiles they were hypocrites, but he sure let it loose with the Pharisees, the equivalent of today's churchgoers. He called them a bunch of snakes, whitewashed sepulchers. Much of their condemnation was based on their reverence of the Law at the expense of all else.

Of course, most of us belong to traditional and denominational churches. And that's good. But we must be on guard: Just because we do not adhere to Sabbath diet rules and the other minute points of the Law does not mean we are safe from the smug self-righteousness of institutionalized religion.

PERPETUAL MOTION

A professional baseball pitcher can throw about 90 miles per hour. Even the fastest pitcher, though, cannot make the ball travel forever. As soon as it leaves his hand, it collides with the air and begins to slow down. Gravity begins sucking it toward the dirt.

The church has been too much like a thrown baseball. It receives a blindingly fresh burst of energy from the Holy Spirit, only to begin to squander it the next day, or the next year. Soon the friction and gravity of rule-lovers begin to undermine the momentum of what the Spirit has initiated. As Paul rebuked the Galatians, "Are you so foolish? Having begun by the Spirit, are you now being perfected by the flesh?" (Galatians 3:3).

Physical organisms grow and change continually, but they end in death. The church, meant to be a spiritual organism, should grow and change indefinitely. It should be the corporate picture of that maturing inner life in each believer. If you and those you walk with are conversing with God in prayer, seeking out his will as a faithful servant, evidence of this should rise to the surface in your church or denomination. The collective friendship with God should change and mature as time goes on. Let's consider some of this evidence more closely.

16 | *Having Spiritual Children*

I REMEMBER dissecting frogs in high school. If the world's best surgeon had wanted to reassemble one of those frogs after I had its guts spread all over the table, he would have thrown up his hands in despair.

Today, the church specializes in Bible dissection. We dissect verses on Sunday morning—often twice, in Sunday school and in a main service. Some churches do it again Sunday night, and again once or twice during the week. Small groups meet for Bible study and practice amateur dissection.

What is the result? Our Bibles are filled with surgical scars in the form of pencil and pen marks that underline verses. Our heads are filled with those excised verses and comments about those verses. But in too many communities, the work of Christ, the application of those verses, remains undone.

This is another hindrance to spiritual growth: *hearing without doing.* Before we finish this chapter, we will examine one final hindrance: *failure to have spiritual children.*

OUT OF THE WALKER

When I was a baby, I was put in a walker. I had progressed from the crawling stage to something better, but it was still not true walking. My mother could have left me in the walker for years, telling me how I would need to balance myself to walk unaided once I was pulled out of the walker. No matter how much she would have taught me, when the day came, I would still not know how to walk. Words are fine, but they can accomplish only so much.

We hear more than we need to in the modern church. We've heard all the clichés—"Practice what you preach" and "Walk the talk"—but somehow the opportunities for practicing and walking seem too rare.

Ask someone on Thursday what was preached on Sunday, and it will take them a few seconds to remember, if they can remember at all. Even the pastor's wife usually won't recall. How about the Sunday before last? Any Sunday from last month?

So many sermons, so little time.

Whom are we kidding? Jesus never said, "Whoever hears these words of mine, buys the cassette, takes lots of notes, and memorizes the theme verse will be like a wise man." This is what he said: "Every one who hears these words of Mine, and acts upon them, may be compared to a wise man, who built his house upon the rock" (Matthew 7:24). The one who hears but does not act will be like a fool. The big rain will come and his house will vanish. That's because words and teaching alone do not make a solid foundation.

I've written before how our church in Argentina many years ago grappled with this problem. We decided that we could not preach a new sermon until the last one was assimilated. In the church at large, that is still a revolutionary idea. In every other area, where people use common sense and expect normal results, it is not.

Will your piano teacher pass you on to the next lesson if you cannot play the current lesson properly? No. "You need more practice," she will say. You may grit your teeth. You may call her terrible things under your breath. But you know she is right. Either you buckle down and learn it, or you might as well quit piano.

Now you both could agree to deceive each other, continue the lessons, and dabble with playing all sorts of music. Then recital day will come. You will have to explain why your fingers will not produce any nice sounds. Blaming it on the piano teacher will not help much.

TEACHING VERSUS ORDERS

If you ask a group of Christians, "Was Jesus a great teacher?" all heads will nod in agreement. I must ask you to pause and reconsider exactly what came out of the Master's mouth. The truth he brought was unquestionably the most important thing the world would ever hear. He was a fine teacher. But I would not be surprised if we measured some modern speakers, with their humor and many vivid examples, and found that they would rate higher as speakers. I say this not to detract from Jesus, because his mission on earth was not to entertain, or solely to teach. He came to save humankind, which meant getting the gospel ball rolling. To do that, *he gave orders*.

If the Bible is a representative reflection of Jesus' teachings, his speeches were fairly short. He was more interested in *training* than *giving speeches*.

Matthew 10 recounts how Jesus gave his disciples authority over unclean spirits and power to heal the sick. But he didn't stop there. He had plans for them to practice the use of this authority:

> These twelve Jesus sent out after instructing them, saying, "Do not go in the way of the Gentiles, and do not enter any city of the Samaritans; but rather go to the lost sheep of the house of Israel. And as you go, preach, saying, 'The kingdom of heaven is at hand.' Heal the sick, raise the dead, cleanse the lepers, cast out demons; freely you received, freely give. Do not acquire gold, or silver, or copper for your money belts, or a bag for your journey, or even two tunics, or sandals, or a staff; for the worker is worthy of his support."
>
> **Matthew 10:5-10**

He said more than this, but you get the idea. The disciples did not shake his hand and tell him, "Oh, what a wonderful sermon, Lord! Such food for thought this week. We'll see you again next Sunday." Instead, they went out and flexed their young spiritual muscles.

Luke 10:17 tells the response of the seventy disciples who had come back from ministering: "Lord, even the demons are subject to us in Your name." Jesus clarifies their thinking about spiritual authority, concluding, "Nevertheless do not rejoice in this, that the spirits are subject to you, but rejoice that your names are recorded in heaven" (Luke 10:20). This should be our pattern for spiritual growth: Receive instruction, practice it, return for adjustments, and go practice some more.

THE STUDY TRAP

This is why we have to be careful with the emphasis we place on sermons and Bible studies. Jesus never said, "Be careful to conduct Bible studies—and make sure you're using the right translation." He said, "*Do* the word of God." When Jesus needed a donkey, he didn't give the apostles a lesson about donkeys, he told them where the donkey was and asked them to go get it.

Once I had to preach five nights in the chapel of a seminary where I was professor of homiletics, which is the art of preparing speeches. My students were going to hear me, so I figured I better lay it on thick so they would know that I know what I'm talking about. I decided to expound each night upon the parable of the Good Samaritan.

One night Jerusalem represented the Garden of Eden; Jericho was the fall of man. The Levite and the Priest in the story represented the religions of this world that didn't help. The Good Samaritan was Jesus, who saved mankind from its fall. Another night Jerusalem was the church, Jericho was the world, the man in trouble was a backslider, and the Good Samaritan was the member of the church that brought him back to church. The third night, Jerusalem was the life in the Spirit, and Jericho was the life in the flesh. And so it went for five nights—new truth, new insights, new depths.

"Brother Ortiz, what a revelation!" the students said. Yet years later I had to repent of dragging others through all those intellectual gymnastics. Jesus did not give the parable for preachers to play games with it.

Is it too simplistic to say the point of the story is that we help those whom we find in need? That's the only thing I *didn't* say in the hours of gab that filled my five sermons.

When I came to understand this truth, I read the passage to my church. I said, "The sermon today is this. When we get out of this place, the first person you find in need, whatever the need is, stop. Meet the need. You are dismissed."

"But Brother Ortiz, we were expecting something deep," some protested. What I had given them was about as deep as the Christian walk gets. If meeting needs was a simple, straightforward matter for Christians, we would see a lot fewer needy people in the world. And a lot more busy Christians.

Now I am not saying that every church should copy what our church did. But just so you'll know, it began to take us two or three months to complete a sermon. Four marching orders in a year—not a bad accomplishment, if you can actually make the teaching a part of your life.

I will have more to say about this tendency to hear but

not to do. But first let's examine one more hindrance to spiritual growth.

GROWTH THROUGH PARENTHOOD

I became a pastor at age 20, and was single until I was 26. As a single pastor, when I saw children misbehaving in church, I thought, "How dare those parents allow this! They don't know how to handle their families. When I have children, they will be better behaved."

I knew everything there was to know about child-raising until God gave me some of my own to raise. Mine, it seemed, were some of the most hyperactive. They taught me tremendous lessons. I could not have matured in this respect unless I became a father. So it is with spiritual maturity—*we cannot grow as we ought to unless we reproduce spiritually* and become involved in the training of young Christians.

Hebrews 5:12 says, "For though by this time you ought to be teachers... you have come to need milk and not solid food." In other words, "You should have children in Christ and you should be feeding them spiritual food."

When you begin to care for someone who is dependent upon you, the act of caring for them tends to curb your own tendency to grumble and complain. When I was a child, I didn't like this shirt, I didn't like those shoes, I didn't like what we were having for dinner, and so on. Then, as I brought up my own children, I began to see myself—and my parents—differently. When Martha and I practically sold our house to finance a trip for our family to California so they could enjoy Disneyland, what did our children say? "We're only going to California? I wanted to go to Hawaii!"

How much this happens in the church. There is never a shortage of murmuring about the schedule of meetings, something offensive in the pastor's last sermon, someone who doesn't deserve to be a deacon, whatever. Much of this hits the pastor, if not directly, then indirectly. He is the church Daddy.

But something different happens when you have people working with the newer believers. When someone is calling you at midnight for advice, laying their troubles on your shoulders, and you are doing your best to follow Galatians 6:2, to "bear one another's burdens," it suddenly seems a little foolish to put on a glum spiritual face and express your concern about whether the pastor's wife wears appropriate clothes to the service.

COVERING THE WHOLE ALPHABET

A few verses after the Hebrews 5 exhortation that "you ought to be teachers," we find this: "Therefore leaving the elementary teaching about the Christ, let us press on to maturity, not laying again a foundation of repentance from dead works and of faith toward God, of instruction about washings, and laying on of hands, and the resurrection of the dead, and eternal judgment" (Hebrews 6:1-2).

Those teachings are good, like a fine steak. But even a steak becomes mundane, and eventually repulsive, if you have it three meals a day, every day. Yet how many of our churches have a slate of basics—our ABC's—that we recycle over and over?

To keep a church fresh, those who have learned ABC should be challenged by learning DEF while also teaching newer Christians ABC. That way no one gets bored and everyone is growing. I once heard of a church that had baptized 1,400 people in a few years, yet the total membership always stayed the same. Some people may have moved, but apparently lots of people got bored. They drifted to another church, or away from the Lord.

So these are some of the hindrances to the growth of the new life of Christ in each of us: living by laws instead of by the new life, being lazy of hearing, being dull of hearing, hearing without doing, and failure to have spiritual children. Before we conclude the book, I want to look more closely at this problem of hearing without doing, which is so pervasive today.

17 | *Is There a Doctrine in the House?*

A YOUNG PREACHER delivered his first sermon as a candidate for the ministry. No one said a thing. He kept waiting for at least some token approval, but nothing happened. Finally he went to an old woman.

"Sister, how did you like my sermon?" he asked.

"I didn't like it for three reasons," she said. "I didn't like it because you read it. Second, I didn't like it because you read it very badly. Third, because it was not worth being read."

We have already seen that hearing is empty if it is not followed by doing. That is not to say that teaching is unimportant. But, like the young preacher, we may need to change the emphasis in what is said—and how it is received. The very nature of church teaching needs re-examination.

SOUND DOCTRINE

The book of Titus has a lot to say about this:

But as for you, speak the things which are fitting for sound doctrine. Older men are to be temperate, dignified, sensible, sound in faith, in love, in perseverance. Older women likewise are to be reverent in their behavior, not malicious gossips, nor enslaved to much wine, teaching what is good, that they may encourage the young women to love their husbands, to love their children, to be sensible, pure, workers at home, kind, being subject to their own husbands, that the word of God may not be dishonored. Likewise urge the young men to be sensible; in all things show yourself to be an example of good deeds, with purity in doctrine, dignified, sound in speech which is beyond reproach, in order that the opponent may be put to shame, having nothing bad to say about us. Urge bondslaves to be subject to their own masters in everything, to be well-pleasing, not argumentative.   Titus 2:1-9

Paul goes on with more explicit instructions in chapter 3:

Remind them to be subject to rulers, to authorities, to be obedient, to be ready for every good deed, to malign no one, to be uncontentious, gentle, showing every consideration for all men. For we also once were foolish ourselves, disobedient, deceived, enslaved to

various lusts and pleasures, spending our life in malice
and envy, hateful, hating one another.   Titus 3:1-3

Paul started off with an encouragement to speak
"sound doctrine." What exactly is that?

I see two kinds of teaching in the Bible. One I call
Christian philosophy. I don't mean philosophy in a secular sense, but as in the pure ethics of Christianity. This
encompasses the things we can talk about, or philoso-
phize about, but cannot really put our hands to. What can
you do about the millennium, except talk—about it?
How can you apply the seven trumpets of Revelation?

The other kind of teaching is Christian doctrine. This
includes the things we can do, the areas where we can
actually change something. For instance, Paul said elderly women should teach younger women how to love
their husbands, how to raise children, how to keep up the
home, how to be frugal with their money, and so on. Are
the elderly women in your church teaching younger ones
about such things? If not, then you're missing out on
sound doctrine in your church.

You might say Paul was speaking to a different culture,
that things are different now. If you live in the United
States or other industrialized nations where divorce is
rampant, where all sorts of social problems can be traced
to the disintegration of family life, then you probably
need the sound doctrine of Titus 2 more than anyone.

"But let us study the Second Coming!" you might say.

Who cares? You cannot change the day of Jesus' return.
But if you have older women and younger women in your
midst, you can get the older ones to help the younger
ones.

IDLE SPECULATION

Sometimes those most inclined to pursue philosophical flights of fancy are those of us in leadership. I was at a seminary for ministers in Puerto Rico when a pastor asked me, "What do you think about the sleeping of the soul?"

Well, I didn't think about it at all. (Of course, everyone who ministers wonders from time to time if those souls seated before him are truly awake or if they've just pasted their eyelids open.)

"What is 'sleeping of the soul'?" I asked.

"When you die, what are you doing from the moment of your death until the day of the resurrection?" he asked.

"I don't know," I said. "I've never been that route before."

Then this person said, quite confidently, "We are awake."

I asked why he had arrived at this conclusion.

"Because the Bible says that those who die are present to the Lord," he said. "That means awake! And Lazarus and the rich man—they were awake on the other side when they were talking to each other."

Then another one says, "No, we are asleep because the Bible says 'Blessed are those who sleep in the Lord because they rest from their work.' And every time the Bible says that somebody died, it says that they were asleep.

"What do you think, Brother Ortiz?"

"I don't think about it because for me, when we die, we are in another dimension of time. For me, the death and resurrection will be simultaneous because when we leave this ground and go to the other side, there is no time. There are no more years and days.

"One thing I know: While we are here, we have to love one another. But as for this sleeping of the soul, let's just wait and see. If God puts us to sleep, we sleep. If he doesn't, we'll be awake. What's the problem?"

The problem, too often for some people, is fretting over issues just like this. Suppose your church votes that you will all be asleep, but it turns out God has ordained that you will be awake. Your vote will not change God's plan. Maybe God will put the workaholics to sleep and the lazy ones he'll keep awake. Who knows?

Paul was not speaking needless words when he wrote Colossians 2:8: "See to it that no one takes you captive through philosophy and empty deception, according to the tradition of men, according to the elementary principles of the world, rather than according to Christ." He wasn't just referring to smooth-tongued Greeks passing off the latest mental candy. He knew that Christianity could become bogged down in the realm of philosophy, of things that could not be absolutely proven and cannot be changed.

This is why our main attention should be on practical doctrine. The Bible has mystery enough to last a lifetime, but it also has more than enough homework assignments to last a lifetime. Jesus' Great Commission was, "Go therefore and make disciples of all the nations, baptizing them in the name of the Father and the Son and the Holy Spirit, teaching them to *observe all* that I commanded you; and lo, I am with you always, even to the end of the age" (Matthew 28:19). This is Christ's doctrine: Go. Make disciples. Baptize them. Teach them to observe all that I commanded you.

The epistles have no shortage of doctrine, either: Husbands, love your wives. Wives, submit to your husbands. Parents, do not provoke your children. Citizens, obey your laws. Visit prisoners. Care for widows and orphans. Meet the needs of the poor.

START WITH RELATIONSHIPS

One reason doctrine should be practical is so that it can bear fruit. Will your neighbor care if she hears that you believe in the millennium? She won't. If your neighbor sees you sacrificing your personal convenience to serve others, and she sees your children are obedient and self-controlled, she may begin to take notice.

I believe that the important things of life, the parts we struggle with, seeking answers to whether we are young or old, concern relationships. A person is always around other people—husband, wife, children, mother-in-law, boss, teacher, the gas station attendant. If you had to pick one word to describe what Jesus died on the cross to heal, it would be relationships. So the following is what you might call a simplified curriculum for relationship-based sound doctrine.

When a person comes to the Lord, his first lesson should concern his relationship with God. The relationship has been broken; now it is fixed, but that is only a beginning. The believer has to learn that he is accepted by God, forgiven completely, that God is "Daddy."

The next lesson addresses the person directly. Sometimes a new Christian has no trouble receiving God's forgiveness, but she doesn't forgive herself. The believer must learn that God has accepted her, not on the basis of performance, but because of the sacrifice of Jesus. If she doesn't learn to forgive herself, she will condemn herself, sort of fighting with herself all the time. She will be so busy with herself that she can do nothing for others.

For the third lesson, look for the next closest relationship. For a man, it is his wife. If the death of Jesus is an adequate basis for God to accept his wife, should that not also be good enough for him? He learns to live with his wife by grace, not by law, not by performance. He learns he must love her as Christ loved the church, which means loving what is imperfect.

Next comes the matter of children. We need to teach parents how to relate to their children, how not to provoke them. For children, we need to teach them how to relate to parents.

THE LOVE LAB

Actually, it is not just children who need instruction on relating to parents. I used to teach elders about the millennium, the tribulation and such things, but those classes didn't truly help anyone.

So I began to teach, "Honor your father and your mother." I gave everyone homework, something concrete to do for their parents. I included myself.

My father was dead, but I called my mother, who was getting very old, and said, "Mom, my wife and I would like you to come and spend a few days with us. In fact, we'd like you to do that every month. And one of those days, I will be your chauffeur, taking you wherever you want from morning till night."

She took me up on the offer. My car was big enough for six people, so she wanted to pick up four of her brothers and sisters. I knew my mom had witnessed to them many times and they still were not Christians, so I suggested she say nothing more and just see what happened.

They decided to go to the place where they grew up— a three-hour drive. Soon they chimed in, "What a son you have! Our children would never take us out like this." We got to the old home and the memories erupted: "Here Mom used to work, here Mom used to talk to neighbors," and so on. They cried and had a wonderful time, and they sort of gave me the credit for this odd treat. When they asked why I did what no one else would do, I said, "Because God said to honor your father and your mother." When we returned that night, they all accepted the Lord.

All I did was try to practice one of the Bible's simple commands, and the fruit poured forth. Let your light shine. People in darkness run toward the light. Jesus understood the process: "Let your light shine before men in such a way that they may see your good works, and glorify your Father who is in heaven" (Matthew 5:16).

We need classes for adults to help them relate to their co-workers, too. For example, we should teach people that to go to the office and look for someone who seems preoccupied. You ask, "What's happened?"

"My wife is very sick," he says. "The doctor says she has to stay in bed. We have three children. But I have to work and I don't know what to do."

So you say, "Tell your wife to stay in bed tomorrow and my wife will take her a hot meal. When we finish working, I will go to your house and we will do the washing, bathe your children, and clean the house."

"You must be kidding," says the worker.

"No, I'm not. This is normal."

Of course, it's not normal for the world. Sooner or later your friend at work, and perhaps others at work, will press you on why you do such things. Tell them it's because God said to love your neighbor as yourself. And you're crazy enough to take that literally.

So you go to your friend's house, do all that you promised, take his wife some flowers and a book, and tell them that a friend of yours will stop by tomorrow to help out.

"You mean there are more of you?" he will ask.

"Oh, yes, we are many."

A RADICAL APPLICATION

When the emphasis is on application of the Bible, you don't need to log a lot of time in church meetings or Bible studies or home groups. I like home groups, but I prefer them in radically different versions.

For example, my wife had a burden for the single women in our church—including not only those who were widows or who had never married, but those whose husbands did not come to church. She picked five of those women to teach, and they helped care for the others.

One of those five was very active, quite a servant. She would come to every service at least forty-five minutes early to clean and prepare the place. She would stay late to pick everything up. She was in church almost every night.

My wife asked her why her husband was not a Christian.

"I preach to him, I put up Scripture plaques every day, but nothing happens," she said.

Martha asked what time she came to church and left most nights, and found that she was gone from 6 to 9. Her husband got home about the time she was leaving, so he normally would eat by himself.

"I leave the meal on the stove and he comes and turns it on and then he eats," the woman said. "Sometimes when I come back, he is asleep."

My wife gave this dear lady a tough first assignment: Do not come to church anymore. It was time to practice 1 Peter 3:1-2: "You wives, be submissive to your own husbands so that even if any of them are disobedient to the word, they may be won without a word by the behavior of their wives, as they observe your chaste and respectful behavior."

The first night her husband thought she was sick. The second night he thought she had quarrelled with the pastor. The third night he asked why she wasn't going to church. She admitted that the pastor and his wife told her to stay home.

"I have to confess that all these years I was a very bad wife. I left you alone so I could go to church. I will now go just one day a week and we should agree together which day it will be." Right away they became much better friends. He even began to escort her to church, though he never would come in.

The woman continued in the class with my wife. Martha tried to teach her how to cook different meals, how to set the table differently, how to behave in bed—

everything you could imagine, they talked about it.

After some weeks, this man said to his wife, "You are a different woman. What happened?"

"Well, I have to confess another little sin," she said. "Though I don't go to church at night, once a week while you are working, some of us meet with the pastor's wife and she is teaching us how to be a good wife."

"Do they have a group where they teach how to be a good husband?" he asked.

Three months later he was baptized. What she hadn't done by her words in thirty years, she did in a matter of months by her deeds.

Where Christian love is practiced, you will not find it dividing people. It brings people together. It heals where no medicine could heal. What does tend to divide, by its very nature, is Christian philosophy, as we'll see next.

18 | *Dividing as We Multiply*

W HEN I HAD FOUR children at home, I had to be many things to them, though I was but one Daddy. One child, for example, was a quiet intellectual; another was an artist.

As I would arrive home each day, David would say, "Daddy, let's play tennis." So we would. Another one would say, "Let's play horses." So I would get on my hands and knees and she would ride me like a horse. There was no problem switching back and forth because I was father to all.

But try to get the siblings to cooperate, and it was another story. A younger daughter would ask David if she could join in our game of tennis.

"Get out of here!" he would say. "You don't know how to play. You miss all the balls."

She'd complain to me. I would tell David to let her play.

"No! She'll spoil the game."

And so it would go. We were one big happy family—until we tried to do something together.

Fortunately, God is a father. He can play horses with the Presbyterians and tennis with the Lutherans. Both groups come away knowing they had fellowship with God.

Unfortunately, God leaves it to those in different denominations to work it out when they want to play with each other. Many games end in a spat. Many games never even start.

I have spent this whole book talking about the God who is so close that he actually lives inside us. He desires continual fellowship with us and longs to see us let that growing relationship spill over into the world as we act on his word. Unless the church functions as a group of people carrying the life of Christ inside them, the unity Christ desired for his bride will never come to pass.

PERFECTED IN UNITY

Something else my children did when they were young was to pray certain prayers very loudly when I was in earshot.

"Lord, you know how we want to go to Disneyland," they would plead.

I think Jesus did something like this the night before his crucifixion. Jesus, who had taught earlier that prayers are usually best done in secret, prayed this out loud and the Holy Spirit saw to it that it became recorded for posterity in Scripture:

"I do not ask in behalf of these alone, but for those also who believe in Me through their word; that they may all be one; even as Thou, Father, art in Me and I in Thee, that they also may be in Us; that the world may believe that Thou didst send Me. And the glory which Thou hast given me I have given to them; that they may be one, just as We are one; I in them, and Thou in Me, that they may be perfected in unity." John 17:20-23

Since Jesus prayed this right before his death, it was sort of a final testament, his will. The mandate for unity is unquestionable. It leaves no room for one denomination or one single church to consider its code or habits or standards to be the end-all of the Christian life. That we are to be one is much, much clearer than any "Thou shalt not smoke" or "Thou shalt not drink wine" or "Thou shalt baptize by immersion."

The very fact that we even have denominations departs from Scripture. You don't find Methodists or Anglicans or Baptists mentioned there. The Bible's only revelation about the structure of the church is that it is both universal and local. The universality of the church is its quality of being worldwide and basically the same, centered on Jesus. The local church is the expression of the universal church in a certain locality. The third dimension —denominations—was added by human beings because of our inability to get along with each other.

LONG DIVISION

Denominations have caused division. I do not exaggerate when I say division in the church is sin. There is only one God, and we have no reason to believe he expected more than one church.

I will go further: It is too kind to say the church is divided. You can divide a number greater than one into other whole numbers—two fives in ten, for example. But you cannot get more than one whole number out of the unity, out of one. Instead, you *break* it into fragments. The church is broken.

Remember the case with the two babies that made Solomon famous? Two women were sleeping in a room with their newborn babies and one woman turned over and accidentally killed her baby. She switched babies with the other woman, and the next day they argued about who was the true mother of the live baby. Solomon said, "Since you can't decide, we'll divide it in two and you can both have a piece."

"Fine," said the deceiving mother.

"No!" said the baby's real mother. "Give him all to her."

Solomon immediately knew that the true mother was the one willing to lay down all self-centered claims for the good of her child. She had higher interests than her own at heart.

Today, we have many Christians who are quick to say, "We can't agree on this or that. We'll just have to divide the church." God would have us adopt the other perspective: "Please, God, give everything to the other party, just don't divide your church."

I am not saying you should give up your belief in the incarnation, the virgin birth, the death and resurrection of Jesus. But many of our differences are not about the heart of our faith, but about peripheral matters: infant baptism, drinking wine, and praying in tongues, for example.

Therefore, when we speak against another church or

denomination, we are hurting ourselves because we belong to the same body. The teeth sometimes accidentally bite the tongue, but the tongue never commands the teeth to leave the body. The tongue forgives the teeth because they are part of the same body. You can pick your friends, but not your brothers and sisters in your family. You are stuck with them. The same is true with our brothers and sisters in Christ.

I am saying strong, idealistic things about denominationalism, but I am also realistic. I know that there is no way we can erase the distinctions between denominations—maybe God can, but we can't. When someone tries to dissolve or seriously change a denomination, he usually ends up starting a new one.

I choose to ignore distinctions between denominations. Though I belong to a denomination, I feel at home in all others. If the Catholics make progress, I say, "Halleluia! *We* are advancing." If the Baptists down the street construct a new building, I say, "*We* have a new building—praise God!"

When I go to a noisy church, I stand up and clap, too. When I go to an Episcopalian service, and I am given the black robes and other trappings, I join their solemn proceedings with joy. When I'm at a charismatic service and they start dancing, I do my best to kick around, too. Like Paul said, "I have become all things to all men" (1 Corinthians 9:22).

You, too, can ignore the differences. It's up to you, and what you harbor in your heart. All Christian churches profess love for Christ, and they can all point to God's blessing on them. So who is anyone to say that they are out of line? God is a father, and he loves all his children.

Our hearts will present many excuses to Jesus' command to love one another. "But they act like they are not saved!" The Bible says to love your neighbors. "But they are my enemies!" Jesus said to love even your enemies. You can't go wrong when you choose to love.

ELUSIVE RIGHTEOUSNESS

When we have difficulty loving those in other denominations because of their dogma, we need to be honest with ourselves. How can we appraise our doctrines as better than another's? If we are really bent on adhering to the intellectual high path of Christian thought and behavior, what makes us so sure our church's teaching is the chosen one? Shouldn't we study in the seminaries of every other denomination to be certain?

Of course, that's impractical. But that's OK. God never intended anyone to serve a lifetime sentence in seminaries. Salvation cannot depend on having the right dogma. *Salvation depends on having the right person.*

To watch the way churches divide over doctrine, you would never think that's the case. You would think that as soon as you get to heaven's gates, St. Peter will say, "Wait a minute. First you need to pass the doctrinal test."

So he gives you a piece of paper and a pencil.

"This is our basic doctrine exam. Ten questions," he says. "If you have seven or more right, you enter right into heaven. If you have four to six right, you go to purgatory for 300 years to receive lessons on doctrine. Less than three, be sure to dress for warm weather."

You nervously accept the pencil and quickly scan the first question.

"Which baptism do you believe in:

    ___ immersion, ___ ablution, ___ sprinkling;

as: ___ an adult, ___ an infant, or ___ other."

You know what your church practiced, but now you wonder if maybe the correct answer isn't something else. So you skip that one for now and read No. 2:

"Are you :

    ___ pre-millennialist, ___ post-millennialist or

    ___ amillennialist?"

Well, heaven will not be like that. You won't take a test on doctrine; instead, Peter will take your pulse. Whoever has the Son, has the life. If Peter is armed with anything, it will be a stethoscope. He'll press it right against your heart.

"I hear a strong beat of love, joy, and peace. Come right in," he'll say.

You say you had all the right beliefs and attended all the church meetings and acted just like the ideal person would act for your denomination? It matters little.

> If I speak with the tongues of men and of angels, but do not have love... And if I have the gift of prophecy, and know all mysteries and all knowledge; and if I have all faith, so as to remove mountains, but do not have love, I am nothing. And if I give all my possessions to feed the poor, and if I deliver my body to be burned, but do not have love, it profits me nothing.
>
> **1 Corinthians 13:1-3**

Nothing means nothing. Lots of religious investment can equal zero profit if you're not careful. How many of us will be surprised when we get to heaven? So many of us will have spent our lives as church busybodies, boning up for our doctrinal exam, only to have Dr. Peter whip out his stethoscope. Don't let your spiritual life get sidetracked on the issues of doctrines that tend only to divide.

In the final chapter, we will conclude this look at doctrine and division, and focus on steps we can take toward healing the problems caused by our sin.

19 ‖ *Peace Is Possible*

MY FATHER DIED when I was a child, leaving my mother with five of us to raise. Amazingly, we were able to buy a house—a fairly nice one, and reasonably priced.

After we moved in, we found out why it was so easy to acquire. In our enthusiasm, we failed to discover that it was beside railroad tracks. Several times an hour, we were treated to "Whooooo! Whooooo! Chugga-chugga-chugga. Whoooo! Whoooo!"

The first week we lost so much sleep that we were nervous, fighting with each other all the time. Then after a few weeks, a strange thing happened—we got used to the sound. We slept peacefully. Of course, visitors couldn't sleep, but that was only a temporary problem.

A few years later, the railway people went on strike, so the trains stopped for a few days. We couldn't sleep! We had grown so accustomed to the noise that we needed it to sleep. Our adjustment, though, did not mean that all that noise was a good thing.

And did you know that people, like trains, can be quite noisy? I'm not talking about people with loud voices, but people consumed with obtrusive things that seem "noisy" because they're unnecessary. Paul wrote that the Christian lacking love is like a "noisy gong or a clanging cymbal" (1 Corinthians 13:1). Likewise, divisions in the church—over a doctrine, or between denominations—grow out of an absence of true love. We may get used to them, but that does not lessen God's displeasure with them.

It's as if a man joined your church and you found out he had been living with ten women for years. So you lovingly say, "Listen, brother, if you want to follow Jesus, you will have to change. You can have only one wife."

"Oh, come on," he says. "I've been doing this for years. We're all used to it. Surely you don't expect me to change at this stage."

None of us can remember when there were no divisions in the church. We cannot roll back the calendar to A.D. 33 and try to circumvent every divisive turn in Christianity's history. But there are some steps we can take to reduce divisions.

DISSOLVING BARRIERS

First, *realize that no difference is beyond change.* No matter how great the division over a particular teaching, no matter how virulently your church or another church lashes out about it, peace can come. It will probably require God's involvement, but he is willing.

Look at the primitive church. Two prominent Christian groups mentioned in the Book of Acts were at Jerusalem and Antioch. The Jerusalem church was very Jewish. They worshiped, paid tithes, and made offerings at the Temple. They circumcised every male baby. They kept all the Jewish feasts. They kept the Mosaic Law. They believed in Christ and continued to try to be perfect Jews. Since their prophets foretold the Messiah, and since Jesus came as one of them, they reasoned that God had not demoted them from being the chosen people with the chosen religion.

Things were different around Antioch. Once God got Peter's attention with a dream, a divinely inspired visit from Cornelius' men, and an outpouring of the Holy Spirit on Gentiles, it finally dawned on him that Jesus was speaking literally when he said he wanted the gospel preached to *all* the earth. So much for an exclusive franchise on being the chosen people.

The church in Antioch started with Gentiles. They knew little or nothing about the Law of Moses, the prophets, and the whole Jewish culture. Jesus, and him crucified, was about all they knew about, which was enough.

As long as Antioch and Jerusalem were well separated, and there were no televised Sunday morning services out of the First Christian Church at Antioch for the Jews to see, everything was fine. The problem arose when a travel agent organized a trip for some Jewish brothers to visit Antioch.

I imagine there was tremendous joy among the

Antioch folks upon their guests' arrival. They hugged each other. They sang, they praised God, they talked about the goodness of the Lord.

After the service, Paul said, "We cannot allow these dear brothers to spend the night down at the local motel. I think everyone should invite them home and practice hospitality." All agreed.

Back at home, one of the Antioch believers might have said, "What would you like for breakfast tomorrow? How about ham and eggs?"

"What! Did you say ham?"

"Why, yes," responded the host.

"But that's unclean," said the visiting Jew.

"No, no, our kitchen is very clean. The Antioch County Health Department checks us every month. Come see."

"You don't understand. Moses forbade us to eat pork."

"Moses?" queried the host. "We don't know that preacher. He never came here."

The Jew leaned his forehead on his palm and stared at the table. He muttered some Hebrew words under his breath. What kind of backwoods hicks had he gotten mixed up with?

"Don't tell me—I bet you don't even have circumcision in Antioch," said the visitor.

"Oh, you want circumcision for breakfast. We've never served that here, but I'll check the gourmet supermarket tonight to see if they stock it. No problem."

"Circumcision is not a breakfast! Abraham circumcised Isaac."

"Abraham? Isaac? Sorry, those preachers haven't been here, either. You know, you guys in Jerusalem have all the big guns. Nobody ever bothers to come out west. We know only Paul and Barnabus."

You get the picture: two very, *very* different Christian cultures. By today's patterns, we would be surprised if they did anything other than form two denominations and never spoke to each other again. But something much different unfolded.

Paul and others returned to Jerusalem and had a council with the elders. At that point, any number of things could have happened. They could have dismissed the Antioch group entirely as a false cult. They could have grudgingly acknowledged the church there as the first new (and of course, inferior) denomination. They could have sent a few scrolls of Law and prophets and a 324-week Bible study course with explicit commands to shape up or ship out. Those would have been man's solutions.

Instead, they drew upon the God who remained close. Not only did they listen with hearts of love to Peter and others who spoke of the new thing God was doing, but in the end "it seemed good to the Holy Spirit and to us to lay upon you no greater burden than these essentials" (Acts 15:28). So they wrote out a few simple requirements, and that was that.

If they can bridge such a wide gap, why can't we cross smaller ones?

WILLING TO SACRIFICE

The fact that we were born into a religious world filled with denominations, that we are used to the clanging of the trains and the clanging of the cymbals in our hearts, is no valid excuse. Division in the church is a sin. How can we correct the adulterer when we tolerate such sin in our midst? We are just as carnal as the adulterer because a carnal self-centeredness lies at the root of our division. We cannot imagine that our own sweet churches could be in error, and we automatically condemn those who differ from us.

What I'm saying is not simply an observation from a church hobbyist. When I discovered how God views division, and how I had participated in this sin, I went to a Trappist monastery for two weeks of fasting and prayer. The Trappists take a vow of silence, except for celebrating Mass. So not only was I praying, but I also was keeping my mouth shut for a change, which was good because God wanted to speak to me.

One day the Spirit did, when I was alone in that big chapel. I went up to the altar and actually laid my body on it.

"Lord, I offer myself as a living sacrifice for the unity of the church. From now on, I die to me, to my denomination, to whatever 'ism' could be in me. And I want to live from here on out for unity. From this mouth will never come any word against any church, any people. I will try to be a bridge. I will start to be a catalytic element of unity within your body."

That was the easy part. Then I had to go home and do something.

For four or five months I taught unity to my congregation, which had grown to about 1,500 people. At the end, I asked, "How many believe that the church is one?"

Many hands went up.

"Put them down. How many of you *really* believe the church is one?"

Even more hands were raised.

"How many of you are willing to prove it? To demonstrate this with your own lives?"

Many hands again.

"Good. Next Sunday, go to the church closest to your house, whether it's Catholic, Lutheran, or Presbyterian. Whatever money you normally spend on gas or bus fare to come here, give it to that church's offering. Only those who live closest to this church come here."

Silence. They didn't want to accept the challenge. But a third of the congregation obeyed.

Eventually we gave two hundred people to the Catholic church, fifty-three to an Anglican church, and others to other churches. Many good things came of this, such as my being invited to speak before many denominations. For example, I was invited to preach in the Church of England missionary convention in England. I was invited to preach at the ordination of a bishop in the Episcopalian church in Latin America.

I am not sharing this as an ordained pattern for church growth. But I want you to see how serious division in the church really is. I want you to sense the sincerity of Jesus' heart as he prayed, "Father, that they might be one!" If this was his parting desire, we cannot be content with less than that.

TAKING POSITIVE STEPS

There are other things we can do to achieve greater unity in the body of Christ. The first one we discussed is to accept that no difference is so great that it cannot be overcome.

Another is *never to speak against any church or congregation.* "Oh, but they're so mistaken on this one point." Don't you suspect that your church is wrong somewhere too, only you don't see it yet? Remember Jesus' admonition about taking the log out of our own eye before you worry about the speck in someone else's eye. One way to view the difference between churches or denominations is that it's not so much a matter of rights here, wrongs there, but of wrongs distributed among all of us.

Another thing is to *forgive.* You think the Episcopalians are too cold? Maybe you're right, maybe you're wrong, but just forgive them anyway. You discern that the Pentecostals jump around too much? Forgive them. Next time, take a coat to the Episcopalian meeting and wear shorts to the Pentecostals' worship. But don't judge them.

If God only accepted us on the basis of our performance, of our adherence to a religious code, we would fail. Likewise, there is no basis for us to judge others, and certainly not by our own flawed understanding of what is exactly right and wrong.

I believe God is trying to regroup his people today. Maybe I should say he's trying to de-group them.

Imagine a man trying to sell his dairy farm. A buyer comes and notices something odd—the cows are separated in six or eight groups. He asks why.

"Oh, we're very organized here," says the farmer. "These cows in this group have shorter legs."

"I see. But the ones in that group have short legs also."

"Yes, but those short-legged cows have longer tails," replies the farmer.

"Ah. But that group over there has cows with short legs and long tails, too. Why are they separate?"

"Because they have long horns."

"Of course. Now that bunch over there has short legs, long tails and long horns. Why are they apart?"

"Because they're white," says the farmer.

Our divisions are just as silly as the farmer's. When we die, there will be only two groups: those who loved one another and those who didn't. The sheep and the goats. God will not be checking a big list of kosher groups and unkosher groups. He will be interested in those who accepted him and shared his love with others. "For I was hungry, and you gave Me something to eat; I was thirsty, and you gave Me drink; I was a stranger, and you invite Me in; naked, and you clothed Me; I was sick, and you visited Me; I was in prison, and you came to Me" (Matthew 25:35-36). If there is any kind of standard God will look at, this is it. "We know that we have passed out of death into life, because we love the brethren" (1 John 3:14).

The best excuses for division amount to clanging cymbals in God's ear. The least we can do, as well as the most we can do, is to love the brethren, and to love those of the world who need to see God's love first-hand. Our fleshly nature jerks at the reins whenever we try. That's why God placed his own life in us. That life remains in us every day, every hour, in church and out of church.

No matter what happens to us in this world, God is enough for us. He promises that he will never leave us. As we surrender to his presence, we will know the joy and the peace and the true adventure of living each day with Jesus Christ, the God who lives and who reigns inside each of us.

Other Books of Interest
from Servant Publications

The Nazarene
Intimate Insights into the Savior's Life
Jamie Buckingham

Any man or woman who has encountered Jesus hungers to know him better. *The Nazarene* invites readers to feast on extraordinary insights into the life of Christ. **$8.99**

"My friend, Jamie, in writing this moving personal account of his insights into the life of our Savior, does not merely tell me about Jesus; he takes me to Him."
— Oral Roberts

A Woman's Guide to Spiritual Warfare
Quin Sherrer and Ruthanne Garlock

Women everywhere face battles that threaten to overwhelm them and those they love. Quin Sherrer and Ruthanne Garlock help readers recognize the tremendous spiritual power God offers them to resist the enemy. It's time for women to take their place in the battle. **$8.99**

"This book is ammunition in the hands of the veteran prayer warrior." — Betty Malz
Author of *Angels Watching Over Me*